Listening to Christmas:

Meditations for the Seasons of
Advent and Christmas

Steven M. Shecley, PhD

Parson's Porch Books

Listening to Christmas: Meditations for the Seasons of Advent and Christmas
ISBN: Softcover 978-1-955581-88-2
Copyright © 2022 by Steven M. Sheeley

Parson's Porch Books is an imprint of Parson's Porch & Company (PP&C) in Cleveland, Tennessee. PP&C is an innovative organization which raises money for the poor by publishing books of noted authors, representing all genres. Its face and voice is **David Russell Tullock**

Parson's Porch & Company *turns books into bread & milk* by sharing its profits with the poor.

www.parsonsporch.com

Listening to Christmas

Contents

Advent Week Three: Joy

Advent Week Four: Peace

Section Two: Listening through Christmas

Foreword

My mother loved Advent and Christmas. She decorated and baked. An Advent calendar was hung on the refrigerator door with magnets, and we took turns opening the cardboard doors each day. We lit the Advent candles, and we sang the hymns, carols, and songs of Christmas.

Later, as an adult, I learned more about the liturgical calendar. With that deeper understanding came a more nuanced view of the Seasons of Advent and Christmas. The ministers and wonderful people of North Broad Baptist Church in Rome, GA, and Northside Drive Baptist Church in Atlanta (Buckhead), GA, introduced me to a worship deeply rooted in the liturgy and lectionary. And, as a dear friend and colleague remarked, "Once you go liturgical, it's hard to go back." The liturgical seasons became far more woven into the fabric of my life.

My mother's death coincided with a change in employment and vocational focus. I was looking for ways to remain connected to my love of biblical scholarship, even though my academic work was almost entirely administrative. Mom had been a prolific writer, and she often submitted entries for the annual Advent devotional booklet published by her church. The first Advent following her death, I edited a group of those devotionals into a booklet published for family members as a way to remember her love of the Seasons. The next spring, unwilling to "give up" anything for Lent, I chose to "take on" writing a daily meditation/musing, using the daily lectionary reading and beginning an email distribution list that has continued to grow. When some on my email list asked if I was planning to repeat those meditations for Advent, it seemed a natural commitment to undertake. Fifteen years later, I am still writing daily meditations/musings on the lectionary readings during the Seasons of Lent and Advent.

Sometimes the daily readings spend less time with Jesus' first Advent than I would like. This volume of meditations and musings on the words to familiar hymns, carols, and songs we hear between Thanksgiving and Epiphany grew out of my desire to do something a little different one year.

9

May the words of these songs and my meditations help us all prepare our hearts and lives for the coming of Jesus the Christ!

Lake Arrowhead, GA
September 2022

Listening to Christmas

More than any other holiday seasons, Advent and Christmas have a "soundtrack." The music of Christmas permeates our lives; after all, the first strains accompany the markdown of any remaining Halloween candy. These seasons may also have their familiar sights, smells, and tastes, but their music and accompanying words evoke some of our most enduring memories and emotions.

On some days the music fades into the background. Even when we should be focused on the words and music of the old familiar carols of the season, we find our minds less engaged than we intended. The seasons of Advent and Christmas tend to be stressful and busy times in our lives. They can be too noisy to allow us the space to find much "peace." We hear the music, but we have trouble really listening.

We try to turn our thoughts to the coming of the Christ child during Advent and Christmas. Many of us set aside some time each day to prepare ourselves to celebrate the incarnation once again. The meditations in this volume are intended to aid that preparation, turning our thoughts to the words of the hymns and carols of these seasons…and sometimes familiar words from the Gospel stories that seem to sing in our ears. Our prayer is that we will find the space to listen.

Section One
Listening through Advent

Advent, Week One
Hope

First Sunday in Advent

O Come, O Come, Emmanuel (vv. 1-2)

Tune: Veni, Emmanuel (Chant)
Translated (Latin): John Mason Neale (1851)

> O come, O come, Immanuel,
> and ransom captive Israel
> that mourns in lonely exile here
> until the Son of God appear.
>
> Refrain
> Rejoice! Rejoice! Immanuel
> shall come to you, O Israel.
>
> O come, Thou Wisdom from on high,
> And order all things, far and nigh;
> To us the path of knowledge show,
> And cause us in her ways to go.

Another season of Advent has arrived. Some of us have been holding out. We have been trying to enjoy the anticipation by waiting until Thanksgiving (or even today) before listening to the music of Advent and Christmas. We have just this weekend begun to exchange our normal household decorations for the "Christmas decorations."

The cries of "Trick or Treat" were still echoing when the world of work and retail flipped the switch to Christmas mode. Candy canes replaced candy corn as the primary seasonal display. And the speakers overhead abruptly switched to the "sounds" of the Christmas season. For many of us these songs evoke warm and cozy feelings. Their notes and lyrics connect us with memories of joyful and happy times, usually spent with family and loved ones.

If we are honest with ourselves, we will probably grow tired of hearing these songs before Christmas finally arrives. Part of that fatigue comes from beginning so early. And the novelty of Grandma getting run over by a reindeer wears off so quickly….

But some of our fatigue with the holiday season is probably due to our failure or inability to pay careful attention. We can all agree that our lives are more "noisy" than they were just a few years ago. We live amidst cacophony. Television and internet "channels" yell at us at full volume, hoping we will boost their ratings by clicking and "liking." Telephones ring and chime and buzz; they are almost impossible to ignore. The noise makes it difficult – at best – to pay attention…to be present and centered. Particularly when the notes and lyrics are already familiar. Particularly when we are supposed to be listening for a "still, small voice."

Today we focus on the first two verses of an ancient chant. Its simple words and haunting melody echo through our lives as they have echoed through sanctuaries for centuries. The first few words remind us that Advent is upon us, as they pray for the advent of Immanuel.

The words speak of a people in exile and captivity. We may, at first, have some difficulty finding ourselves numbered among the captives and exiles. And we may want to think only in historical terms of the biblical people. But as we quiet ourselves, we can easily think of facets of our living that hold us captive. We can contemplate people in our lives from whom we feel estranged. And we can see the ways in which we feel separated from God and God's reign.

The plaintive chant of medieval monks resonates in our lives. It cancels some of the noise that surrounds us each day. And we, too, begin to pray that the Son of God would come to ransom us from our exile and captivity.

The second verse invites the guiding presence of Wisdom "from on High." The ancient Hebrews, probably influenced by Greek thought, began to connect the idea of Wisdom to the concept of God's Spirit/breath. Wisdom is the most prominent female persona of the godhead, the Spirit which gives vitality and direction to human living.

Our Advent prayer began by inviting salvation into our lives and our world. It continues with an invitation to God's guidance and expresses our desire for the ability to follow the path of God's knowledge and wisdom.

Another season of Advent has arrived. We welcome the season with anticipation. And we pledge ourselves to pay attention. Come, Lord Jesus.

May God's Spirit open our eyes to see and our ears to hear. This day and every day. Amen.

First Monday in Advent

Come, Thou Long Expected Jesus, (v. 1)

Words: Charles Wesley
Tune: HYFRYDOL

Come, thou long expected Jesus,
born to set thy people free;
from our fears and sins release us,
let us find our rest in thee.
Israel's strength and consolation,
hope of all the earth thou art;
dear desire of every nation,
joy of every longing heart.

The Christian life is lived between the "already" and the "not yet." Each year, the season of Advent provides clear reminders of our in-between existence. Once again, we await the appearance of Jesus the Savior…even as we are aware that his incarnation lies in the now ancient past.

The first verse of Wesley's familiar hymn reminds us of our kinship with those ancient Hebrews. Their calendar was organized around festivals, high holy times that celebrated and gave thanks for the gifts of a gracious God in their world. These festivals also gave voice to their longing for cosmic redemption and political salvation. In fact, they probably would have been quite happy settling for a little political and cultural salvation. Constantly beset by external enemies, the history of Israel is filled with the desire for a safe space to live and work and worship.

They looked to Heaven for the appearance of a Messiah. They remembered the glory days of David and Solomon and prayed that YHWH would one day restore the Davidic throne. And they waited….

There are days when the Christian faithful look back to the events captured in the narratives of the four Evangelists and dream of the glory days of God's Messiah. Like the ancient Hebrews, we sometimes wonder if God has forgotten the cosmos. Or if Jesus will ever return to complete the redemptive process begun in Bethlehem, accomplished on Golgotha, and sealed in Jerusalem's Upper Room. We allow our fears and sins to hold us captive. We lock our faith in the past and forget the faithfulness of our God demonstrated throughout the ages.

If we are not vigilant, our fears rob us of hope. If we are not faithful, our anxieties rob us of joy.

We live in the time between the "already" of Jesus' incarnation and the "not yet" of Jesus' return. We are not the first; we may not be the last. The season of Advent will always highlight our unresolved existence. But Advent will also remind us to invite the hope and joy of Jesus' rest and consolation into our unresolved lives. And, perhaps, give us the space to hear and feel the presence of God's Spirit already present with us.

May the Spirit of God give us strength and stamina for the living of these days. This day and every day. Amen.

Lo, How a Rose E'er Blooming

Translator: Theodore Baker
Tune: ES IST EIN ROS – Michael Praetorius

Lo, how a Rose e'er blooming
From tender stem hath sprung!
Of Jesse's lineage coming
As men of old have sung.
It came, a flower bright,
Amid the cold of winter
When half-gone was the night.

Isaiah 'twas foretold it,
The Rose I have in mind:
With Mary we behold it,
The virgin mother kind.
To show God's love aright
She bore to men a Savior
When half-gone was the night.

This Flower, whose fragrance tender
With sweetness fills the air,
Dispels with glorious splendor
The darkness everywhere.
True man, yet very God,
From sin and death He saves us
And lightens every load.

The tune has a medieval feel; we can almost see the singers dressed in tights and doublets. The words match the haunting notes that seem to die away at the end of every verse. They remind us that the season of Advent finds its roots in the story of David and David's reign. These words speak of a splash of color amidst the cold, dreary white of winter. Not the crisp white of a new snowfall under the winter sun. But rather the bleak white of the dead of winter under the half-light of a cloudy sky.

We do not expect to see the vivid red of a blooming rose. We thought, perhaps, that the rose bush was dead. We assumed that the ground was too cold or too barren for the rose's stem to produce a flower, just as the ancient Hebrew people worried that the lineage of Jesse was too far in the past and too wizened by the years to produce a Messiah.

Isaiah the prophet found himself and his hearers in the dreary darkness of exile. They were far from Judea, far from God, and faced with the reality of the defeat of David's kingdom. But the word of YHWH came to him again and again, and he discovered a sense of hope, even among the ruins of Solomon's Temple. The people of YHWH found their sense of hope in Isaiah's words, even in the darkness of exile.

We hear the amazing words of the archangel with Mary. They promise a new bloom after what seems an eternity of waiting and hoping. They assert her impending – and miraculous – pregnancy. They assure her and all who are listening in to the Evangelist's story that this miraculous son will save God's cosmos.

With the advent of Jesus comes the promise of the morning. With the advent of Jesus comes the promise of the spring. The miraculous rose, blooming in the night of dying winter, promises the light of God's love and presence. And the lightening of our load.

Humans have been talking about salvation throughout our entire existence. Our words to describe and discuss the sacred have, perhaps, become too familiar and too comfortable. The season of Advent comes each year to restore our sense of wonder and reconnect us with the miraculous and mysterious. It invites us to see our world through the rose-colored glasses of hope.

May God's Spirit guide us to see the world with wonder. This day and every day. Amen.

First Wednesday in Advent

Let All Mortal Flesh Keep Silence (vv. 1-2)

Words: Liturgy of Saint James
Tune: PICARDY

Let all mortal flesh keep silence,
and with fear and trembling stand;
ponder nothing earthly minded,
for with blessing in His hand
Christ our God to earth descendeth,
our full homage to demand.

King of kings, yet born of Mary,
as of old on earth He stood,
Lord of lords, in human vesture -
in the body and the blood.
He will give to all the faithful
His own self for heavenly food.

Silence is difficult to find during the holidays. Our already "noisy" lives get even more hectic as we shop and eat and drink our way through the days between Thanksgiving and New Year's. But reverence often demands some silent space, a place where we can quiet ourselves and pay mindful attention.

The season of Advent calls us to consider our place in the cosmos. Turning our attention to the presence of the Divine enfleshed calls us to slow down and contemplate…even if we can devote only a few moments at a time. That contemplation confirms at least two conclusions for us. First, we occupy a relatively humble place in the cosmic order. We would not be surprised, in fact, if most of our existence escaped God's attention. Secondly, we are not alone. God has always been powerfully present with us in our world, and the gift of Jesus is the ultimate sign of God's presence and saving grace.

Even our momentary achievement of silence allows us to realize the transcendent power of an all-capable God. We are probably too guilty – especially during Advent and Christmas – of reducing Jesus to the image of the swaddled and feed-boxed infant. That image makes Jesus the child warm and comfortable, and we are thankful that he has the protection of his young parents (along with the angels, shepherds, and magi).

We remember, though, that we live in the in-between. The baby in the manger is also the adult on the cross and the risen Savior in the upper room and beyond. We stand in the middle and contemplate what it means that the long-awaited God-child became both servant and king, as we await his return from the Heavenly realms.

That ancient Advent promises the future Advent. And both rest on the ongoing presence of God with us.

We have programmed ourselves to look for God's presence only in the miraculous and magnificent, forgetting or ignoring the biblical passages that reveal God's presence in the small and the still. One of the great ironies of the seasons of Advent and Christmas is how easily we can miss God's presence. So, this day we stop to heed the words of the hymn that admonish all those of mortal flesh to "keep silence" and experience the peace and hope of God's presence.

May God's Spirit guide us to the spaces of reverent silence in our lives. And give us hope. This day and every day. Amen.

First Thursday in Advent

For Unto Us a Child is Born

From *Messiah*
G. F. Handel

For unto us a Child is born, unto us a Son is given,
and the government shall be upon His shoulder;
and his name shall be called Wonderful Counsellor,
the Mighty God, the Everlasting Father,
the Prince of Peace.
(Isaiah 9:6)

The strings and voices dance their way through this setting of Isaiah's words in Handel's *Messiah*. The words of Isaiah's prophecy spoke of a royal son, an heir to the throne of David born at just the right time for a nation beset by enemy armies. They were powerful words of hope for a people wondering if YHWH had forgotten them. For here, in the birth of the King's son, they had the answer to their questions of survival. A son had been born "unto us." God had given a son to take on the mantle of government.

Isaiah was likely a little more far-sighted than his ancient hearers. The ancient Hebrews rejoiced in the thought that the royal line had been saved from extinction through the birth of a son to continue ruling from the Davidic throne. But we know the history of the nations of Israel and Judah. We are all too aware of their conquest and exile…and the dispersion of the Hebrew people throughout the Greco-Roman world.

The word of YHWH came to Isaiah – for his hearers and beyond. After all, it was a word from God. Alive and active. Applicable for all of God's people. The folks who preserved, interpreted, and re-interpreted Isaiah's prophetic words were still looking for the promised Child. They were still hoping for the son given from God who would re-establish the throne of David in all of its glory and power and righteousness. They heard these hopeful words anew by the banks of the Tigris and Euphrates rivers, trapped in a Babylonian exile. They repeated the words of hope to the cadence of invading Roman soldiers, desperately hoping for a Messiah to bring God's government and God's peace to replace the *"pax" Romana.*

Isaiah's words – set to Handel's music – remind us that our lives of faith and hope are lived in the in-between. Despite the cosmic victory accomplished by Jesus on Golgotha's cross, our world continues to contend with wars and rumors of wars. Cosmic and natural "evil" is still too present with us. And far too many of us seem to ignore the "Prince of Peace," even when we claim to follow him and his commandments.

Still, Isaiah's words give us hope, just as Handel's notes propel our hearts and spirits upwards. We are a people of hope and faith. We are a people for whom the darkness has been lifted, dispelled by the great light of Jesus' birth, life, death, and resurrection. Even though we live in the in-between, the promise of the first Advent has been fulfilled. So we sing, and we dance and we join our voices with the cosmic refrain: Wonderful Counsellor, Mighty God, Everlasting Father, Prince of Peace!

May God's Spirit open our eyes and ears to hear the words of the prophet anew. And may our hope be renewed in the promise and the presence of the one who is the Prince of Peace! This day and every day. Amen.

First Friday in Advent

Gabriel's Message

Basque Carol (13th/14th Century)
Translator: Sabine Baring-Gould

The angel Gabriel from heaven came,
his wings as drifted snow, his eyes as flame;
"All hail," said he to meek and lowly Mary,
"most highly favored maiden." Gloria!

"I come from heav'n to tell the Lord's decree:
a blessed virgin mother you shall be.
Your Son shall be Immanuel, by seers foretold,
most highly favored maiden." Gloria!

Then gentle Mary meekly bowed her head;
"To me be as it pleases God," she said.
"My soul shall laud and magnify his holy name."
Most highly favored maiden, Gloria!

Of her, Immanuel, the Christ, was born
In Bethlehem, all on a Christmas morn,
and Christian folk throughout the world will ever say,
"Most highly favored maiden." Gloria!

She was just a young peasant girl. Nothing about her should have caused anyone to give her a second thought or notice her at all. Stories would be written about her many years later. After all, she would become a central figure in Christianity. When Luke's Gospel introduces her, though, she is still living with her parents and waiting out the time period between betrothal and her marriage to Joseph.

It was a very awkward time for her to be awakened by Gabriel's nocturnal visit and his message. No one in her life would be pleased by Gabriel's announcement. Her family's worst fears would come to fruition; her intended husband would be well within his rights to accuse her of adultery. At best, she would be the cause of overwhelming shame to her family. At worst, Joseph could demand that she be executed.

Earlier in Luke's Gospel, Zechariah had reacted to Gabriel's appearance and good news with amazement and disbelief. In stark contrast, Mary reacted with calm acceptance. Her questions are simple and logical, and she demonstrated a clear grasp of the realities. More than that, her faithful reaction is worthy of the great figures in biblical history. Gabriel's affirmation of God's power is met by her immediate obedience. God is present, and the impossible will be almost commonplace.

The words of the Basque carol have a gentle rhythm. It would be very easy to walk and sing this song at the same time. The first two verses paraphrase and summarize Gabriel's message delivered to Mary and announcing that she has been chosen to bear God's Son. Verse three borrows words from Mary's song later in the chapter, although her response to Gabriel could easily be seen as prelude to her response to Elizabeth (the *Magnificat*). The final verse speaks of Immanuel's birth in Bethlehem.

The song's refrain repeats Gabriel's characterization of Mary as "most highly favored maiden." The juxtaposition with various references in the song to Mary as "meek and lowly" and "gentle" continues to remind us that the entire encounter has a surreal quality. Perhaps they are also a reminder of the Gospel's theme that virtue is found among the poorest and lowest of society and that Jesus has come to turn everything upside down.

May the presence of God's Spirit remind us that nothing is impossible anymore. And may our faithfulness be that of Mary. This day and every day. Amen.

First Saturday in Advent

Magnificat (Luke 1)

My soul magnifies the Lord, and my spirit rejoices in God my Savior, for he has looked with favor on the lowliness of his servant. Surely, from now on all generations will call me blessed; for the Mighty One has done great things for me, and holy is his name. His mercy is for those who fear him from generation to generation. He has shown strength with his arm; he has scattered the proud in the thoughts of their hearts.

He has brought down the powerful from their thrones, and lifted up the lowly; he has filled the hungry with good things, and sent the rich away empty. He has helped his servant Israel, in remembrance of his mercy, according to the promise he made to our ancestors, to Abraham and to his descendants forever (Luke 1:46-55).

Since Matthew and Luke are the only canonical gospels to explore the events surrounding Jesus' birth, many of the biblical passages we read during the seasons of Advent and Christmas are found in the first few chapters of their narratives. Each evangelist tells the story from a different perspective. Matthew's Gospel emphasizes Jesus' connection with the ancient Hebrew traditions. Matthew's Joseph, like the Joseph of Genesis, has vivid dreams through which God communicates clearly.

Luke's story of Jesus' birth, though, often unfolds through the experiences and thoughts of Mary. And angels. Many angels. God's Archangel – Gabriel – is quite busy as Luke's Gospel begins. First, he appears to Zechariah in the Temple with a message of God's miraculous blessing too fantastic for Zechariah to accept or believe. Next, we see Gabriel appearing to Mary while the rest of the household is fast asleep, announcing to her that she was about to become a mother. The conversation between Gabriel and Mary is, if anything, even more surreal than the one Zechariah experienced. She has every bit as many questions about the nature of this impending blessing, and she seems less intimidated by the angelic presence than the aging priest. More to the point, however, she is quick to proclaim her obedience to the will of God.

We can only imagine the reaction of her family to the strange news of her immaculate conception. What Luke tells us is that she is quickly shipped off to visit her older relative Elizabeth, herself newly and miraculously pregnant. Like Luke's readers, we are not surprised. We are competent readers of biblical texts, and we know that God's plans have often been accomplished through resilient and faithful women during the history of the Hebrew people. When Mary arrives to stay with Elizabeth and Zechariah, Elizabeth is already in the second trimester of her pregnancy. And, at Mary's greeting, Elizabeth's child "leaps" in utero. Elizabeth, "filled with the Holy Spirit," greets her young kinswoman as "blessed."

And Mary bursts into song.

We name her song "Magnificat" from the first word of the Latin translation. It is a song of praise and thanksgiving that the time had come for God to effect deliverance for the children of Israel. It is a song of gratitude that the time had come for the promises of Hebrew Scripture to be accomplished. The setting is dramatic and theatrical, and even more powerful for being so. Mary's song soars. Elizabeth has termed her "blessed," and all generations to come will call her "blessed." Her words admit her humility; only through this unimaginable gift of God's grace would someone of her lowly socio-economic status be so exalted. Only the reality of God's presence and power will redeem the shame resulting from her unwed pregnancy. Only the holiness and mercy and mighty power of God redeems this situation.

The themes in her words will be taken up and repeated throughout Luke's Gospel. In the life and words of Jesus we will often encounter the idea that the reign of God overturns what society considers normal. The poor and hungry will have seats at the banquet table, and the rich will walk away empty and unfilled. God's strength will topple kings and princes from their thrones and exalt the humble. The last shall be first, and the first shall be last.... The history of the Hebrew people was a long history of persecution and exile. They had been a poor, wandering people in a strange land. Luke's story of Jesus is set to unfold, and Mary's song – her Magnificat – sets the stage for what we should expect.

Unlike many of the other songs of Advent and Christmas, Mary's words will likely not evoke notes or a tune in our ears. But her words resonate with our hearts and souls as we anticipate both the birth and second Advent of Jesus. As we join our voices with hers to sing of the mercy, grace, and power of God.

May God's Spirit renew our songs of praise and thanksgiving. This day and every day. Amen.

Advent Week Two

Love

Second Sunday in Advent

Love Came Down at Christmas

Words: Christina G. Rossetti (1885)
Music: GARTON (Traditional Irish Melody)

Love came down at Christmas,
Love all lovely, Love divine;
Love was born at Christmas;
star and angels gave the sign.

Worship we the Godhead,
Love incarnate, Love divine;
worship we our Jesus,
but wherewith for sacred sign?

Love shall be our token;
Love be yours and Love be mine;
Love to God and others,
Love for plea and gift and sign.

The words of Rosetti's poem were set to music to serve as a Christmas hymn/carol. Her "other" Christmas poem/carol ("In the Bleak Midwinter") is better known, but that may have more to do with its familiar musical setting. Rosetti was deeply religious, and she included this poem in a volume entitled *Time Flies: A Reading Diary* (1885), as the entry for Dec. 29. The poem first appeared as a hymn in the early 20th century.

Her simple words evoke both a cozy warmth and a quiet power. They likely take their theme from the Gospel and letters of John. 1 John, in particular, argues that love for God and for one another is the defining characteristic of a believer and the faith community.

The first stanza evokes both manger and shepherds' field. Love's incarnation – divine love come in human form and flesh – came to Earth on that first Christmas day. God's love was "born," and the heavens declared his birth in star and song.

Stanza two reminds us of Charles Wesley's majestic hymn "Love Divine, All Loves Excelling," but their simplicity paints a picture that is somehow warmer and quieter…if no less powerful. Like Wesley's hymn, though, Rosetti's words turn our attention to incarnate love's divinity. The words embody our worship of the Godhead and proclaim our worship of Jesus. The stanza concludes with a salient question: what will be the "sacred sign" of our worship?

The final stanza answers that question. Nothing less than love for God and love for each other will provide the "sacred sign" to others that we are part of the faithful. Believers have been called to love one another in imitation of God's love for us. Our love marks us as recipients of God's love. Only our love for God and others argues for our true identity. It is sign to the world and gift to all who receive Jesus.

Those who have had the privilege of holding a newborn baby will quickly testify to the immediate and overwhelming feelings of love and wonder they experienced. We would be surprised if Joseph and Mary did not feel that love for their newborn baby, even in the midst of the amazing and exhausting events of that first Christmas. Rosetti's words remind us, as well, that the gift of Jesus' human presence is a tangible sign of God's love for us. The baby in Bethlehem's manger, welcomed by star and angel, binds us all in God's love.

May our lives be swaddled in the love of God. This day and every day. Amen.

Second Monday in Advent

While Shepherds Watched Their Flocks

Words: Nahum Tate (1700)
Tune: WINCHESTER OLD or CHRISTMAS (Handel)

While shepherds watched their flocks by night,
all seated on the ground,
an angel of the Lord came down,
and glory shone around.

"Fear not," said he for mighty dread
had seized their troubled mind
"glad tidings of great joy I bring
to you and all mankind.

"To you, in David's town, this day
is born of David's line
a Savior, who is Christ the Lord;
and this shall be the sign:

"The heavenly babe you there shall find
to human view displayed,
all simply wrapped in swaddling clothes
and in a manger laid."

Thus spoke the angel. Suddenly
appeared a shining throng
of angels praising God, who thus
addressed their joyful song:

"All glory be to God on high,
and to the earth be peace;
to those on whom his favor rests
goodwill shall never cease."

The words of this hymn come from a time when most of the hymns sung by English congregations took their text from the Psalms. The biblical Psalms would be paraphrased in order to give them a poetical form more suited to English, complete with rhyme and meter. One goal was to remain as faithful to the biblical text as possible, but it was balanced by the desire to have a text that could comfortably be sung. This hymn is one of the few that applied that metrical philosophy to a text that wasn't a Psalm.

The result is a hymn text that stays relatively true to Luke's nativity narrative. Its verses focus on the experience of the shepherds in the fields outside of Bethlehem on the night of Jesus' birth. Luke's words, especially in their King James Version translation, are very familiar to us. They resonate deeply with us, and they engender feelings of both comfort and excitement.

Most of us are familiar with the first televised special based on the cartoons of Charles Schultz. "A Charlie Brown Christmas" first aired in 1965, and it brought Schultz's beloved characters into our living rooms during prime time. It featured the musical stylings of the Vince Guaraldi Trio, and the songs included in the special have maintained their popularity over the years. The show's plot revolves around Charlie Brown's seasonal depression and centers on the theme that Christmas has become too commercialized and lost its true meaning. Lucy suggests that Charlie Brown find a worthwhile activity to take his mind off his melancholy, but that experience only serves to reinforce the idea that the true meaning of the Christmas season has been lost. At the height of his despair and frustration, Charlie Brown wonders loudly if anyone knows what Christmas is all about.

Linus, blanket clutched close, walks to the center of a now-quiet stage. He assures Charlie Brown and the rest of the neighborhood kids that he knows what Christmas is all about. With the spotlight isolating him at center stage, Linus recites the words that begin Luke 2.

It is a stunningly powerful moment. Luke's are familiar words, and we read them every Christmas. If we ensure that we *hear* them, though, everything else drops away. We are transported in time and place and find ourselves sitting around the small fire with the other sleepy shepherds. Like them, we are shocked and frightened by the sudden and terrifying appearance of God's archangel in our midst. We have only just been able to catch our breath when the angelic chorus overawes us again.

"All glory be to God on high, and to the earth be peace…." These are words that deserve to be sung, even if our voices do not quite match those of the chorus of angels. God's peace has come into our midst in the form of a human child. God's eternal "goodwill" will rest on God's good creation, now and forevermore.

May God's Spirit put the song of God's glory in our hearts and on our lips. And find us ever faithful. This day and every day. Amen.

Second Tuesday in Advent

Thou Didst Leave Thy Throne

Words: Emily E. S. Elliot (1864)
Tune: MARGARET [Timothy R. Matthews (1876)]

Thou didst leave Thy throne and Thy kingly crown,
When Thou camest to earth for me;
But in Bethlehem's home was there found no room
For Thy holy nativity.
O come to my heart, Lord Jesus,
There is room in my heart for Thee.

Heaven's arches rang when the angels sang,
Proclaiming Thy royal degree;
But of lowly birth didst Thou come to earth,
And in great humility.
O come to my heart, Lord Jesus,
There is room in my heart for Thee.

The foxes found rest, and the birds their nest
In the shade of the forest tree;
But Thy couch was the sod, O Thou Son of God,
In the deserts of Galilee.
O come to my heart, Lord Jesus,
There is room in my heart for Thee.

Thou camest, O Lord, with the living word
That should set Thy people free;
But with mocking scorn, and with crown of thorn,
They bore Thee to Calvary.
O come to my heart, Lord Jesus,
There is room in my heart for Thee.

When the heavens shall ring, and the angels sing,
At Thy coming to victory,
Let Thy voice call me home, saying "Yet there is room,

There is room at My side for thee."
My heart shall rejoice, Lord Jesus,
When Thou comest and callest for me.

Emily E.S. Elliot was committed to the rescue missions and Sunday Schools of Victorian England. As part of her work with those Christian charities, she wrote a number of hymns for children. They often seem designed to help the children in the Sunday School learn about the life of Jesus.

Elliot's words illuminate the stark contrast between Jesus' true heavenly identity and his earthly realities. Coming from the heavenly throne room, he and his parents found no accommodations in Bethlehem. The halls of heaven "rang" with songs acclaiming his royalty, but his birth took place in the humblest of earthly circumstances. The birds and animals on earth had somewhere they could call home, while Jesus wandered from town to town. His divine message of freedom was scorned and ignored; Jesus was crucified with his only crown being a crown of painful thorns.

And throughout the song comes a refrain: "there is room in my heart for thee."

The challenge to our modern ears, particularly to those of us raised in an evangelical tradition, is to overcome the familiarity of that refrain. We run the danger of being so comfortable with the idea of a personal relationship with Jesus – of "inviting" Jesus "into our hearts" – that we might not actually contemplate the continuing power of such an invitation.

The children of Great Britain's industrial age probably knew too well what it felt like to be poor and homeless and hungry. They knew what it was to have hopes and dreams with no concept of how any of them might come to fruition. But they could sing about offering Jesus – both infant and adult – the only "room" they had to give…the "room" in their hearts. Most of us, on the other hand, have known little in the way of insecurity when it comes to food or shelter. We often have overflowing resources we could offer. But we, too, may find that our most powerful resource we can offer Jesus

– both the child and the risen Lord – is the "room" in our hearts.

May God's Spirit be powerfully present in us and among us. And show us how to love God and each other. This day and every day. Amen.

Second Wednesday in Advent

Gesù Bambino

Pietro Yon (1917)
Translator: Frederick H. Martens

When blossoms flowered 'mid the snows
Upon a winter night,
Was born the Child, the Christmas Rose,
The King of Love and Light.

The angels sang, the shepherds sang,
The grateful earth rejoiced;
And at His blessed birth the stars
Their exultation voiced.

O come let us adore Him,
O come let us adore Him,
O come let us adore Him,
Christ the Lord.

Again the heart with rapture glows
To greet the holy night,
That gave the world its Christmas Rose,
Its King of Love and Light.

Let ev'ry voice acclaim His name,
The grateful chorus swell.
From paradise to earth He came
That we with Him might dwell.

O come let us adore Him,
O come let us adore Him,
O come let us adore Him,
Christ the Lord.

One drawback to being a biblical scholar rather than a church historian is a tendency to look first for connections to stories in the Bible. Frankly, neither the Hebrew Bible nor the Christian New Testament will offer much help with the opening lines of this carol. The "roots" of the image of Jesus as the "Christmas Rose" lie, instead, in an ancient legend about a shepherd girl named Madelon. She stood in the snow outside the stable, watching everyone from her fellow shepherds to the Magi bringing gifts to the newborn child. Being very poor, though, she had no gift of her own to present. And she wept. An angel watched her weeping and was moved to help her. The angel caused the snow at Madelon's feet to vanish; as it melted, a beautiful white flower with pink tips appeared. Overjoyed, Madelon brought her gift of this wonderful flower to the holy family.

Christmas roses – like their Lenten relatives – are not part of the rose family. They are, rather, hellebores. They grow in central Europe, and they bloom in the winter…around Christmas time. The white blooms represent purity, and the pink/red parts of the flowers are easily aligned with Jesus' suffering. The plant is an evergreen, another common connection to the Christmas season and Jesus' eternity.

The song itself celebrates the birth of the baby Jesus. Like the Christmas rose flower, the holy baby was born in the midst of winter. The "Lord of Love and Light" "bloomed" forth amidst the cold and bitter snows. One of the joys of this song is that what looks like the second verse is set to slightly different music, allowing both the notes and the words to rise when the text speaks of angels and shepherds singing and the "grateful earth" rejoicing. The same pattern also highlights the fourth "verse," which calls us all to join the "grateful" chorus and acclaim Jesus' name. Between the verses, a chorus echoes the refrain of the majestic "O Come, All Ye Faithful."

We will not find Madelon, the poor shepherd girl, in the infancy narratives of Matthew or Luke. She is the stuff of legend, and her Christmas rose is not native to Bethlehem. Her story might resonate with us, though, especially in this season when we contemplate the enormity of God's gift in the birth of Jesus. We could easily conclude that we had no gift of our own to present to the Christ child. This carol calls us to give the gift of our voices and hearts, to swell the "grateful" chorus that sings praises to Jesus. Its words bid us come and return God's love with our own adoration.

May God's Spirit fill our hearts with love, giving voice to our grateful adoration. And find us faithful. This day and every day. Amen.

Second Thursday in Advent

There's a Song in the Air

Josiah G. Holland (1872)

There's a song in the air!
There's a star in the sky!
There's a mother's deep prayer
and a baby's low cry!
And the star rains its fire
while the beautiful sing,
for the manger of Bethlehem
cradles a King!

There's a tumult of joy
o'er the wonderful birth,
for the virgin's sweet boy
is the Lord of the earth.
Ay! the star rains its fire
while the beautiful sing,
for the manger of Bethlehem
cradles a King!

In the light of that star
lie the ages impearled;
and that song from afar
has swept over the world.
Every hearth is aflame,
and the beautiful sing
in the homes of the nations
that Jesus is King!

We rejoice in the light,
and we echo the song
that comes down through the night
from the heavenly throng.
Ay! we shout to the lovely
evangel they bring,
and we greet in his cradle
our Savior and King!

Few events are as fraught with risk as giving birth. Perhaps that explains, in part, why such a common occurrence is met with such uncommon joy. Nothing else feels quite the same as the burst of love and affection that comes with holding a newborn baby. First-time parents worry about a host of things. One of those worries that keeps them up at night is wondering whether the love they have for each other will expand sufficiently to encompass another family member. That's certainly one worry that disappears when the baby arrives.

This poetic text draws two scenes. One scene looks into the stable with its manger, the baby Jesus, and his exhausted parents. Like many babies, Jesus cries; like many mothers, Mary answers Jesus' crying with a lullaby. One of the songs "in the air" is Mary's soothing hum…and her "deep prayer." We have very little idea what kinds of thoughts occupied the minds of Mary and Joseph as the night and next few days unfolded. We can surmise that there were many "deep prayers" offered to God.

The other scene in this text is the hillside outside of Bethlehem, alive with the angelic chorus and the brightness of the Christmas star. That scene, and its cosmic implications, dominates the rest of Holland's poem. The text is full of references to the brightness of the star. It "rains its fire" while the angels sing and offer their "tumult of joy." In the poet's imagination, the star's light stretches across "impearled" ages, and the ancient "song from afar" has reached every corner of the world. Every household's "hearth" is now "aflame," and every voice echoes the song of the angels. Our voices join theirs in proclaiming the good news ("evangel") that Bethlehem's manger "cradles" "our Savior and King."

There is still a song in the air, and it is the song of love and joy. We fill our homes with light and music during this season of Advent. Both somehow push back the darkness that comes as the sun sets earlier each evening. Both somehow offer warmth as the days grow colder. Both call us to share the joy of the coming Christ child, as well as our love for God and for each other.

May God's Spirit light our lives and help us lift our voices in love and praise. And find us faithful. This day and every day. Amen.

Second Friday in Advent

Wexford Carol (Enniscorthy Carol)

Tune: Traditional Irish Carol (12th Century?)
Words: English (19th-20th Century?) – Collected by William Grattan
Flood

Good people all, this Christmas time,
Consider well and bear in mind
What our good God for us has done
In sending his beloved son
With Mary holy we should pray,
To God with love this Christmas Day
In Bethlehem upon that morn,
There was a blessed Messiah born.

The night before that happy tide,
The noble Virgin and her guide
Were long time seeking up and down
To find a lodging in the town.
But mark right well what came to pass
From every door repelled, alas,
As was foretold, their refuge all
Was but a humble ox's stall.

Near Bethlehem did shepherds keep
Their flocks of lambs and feeding sheep
To whom God's angel did appear
Which put the shepherds in great fear
Arise and go, the angels said
To Bethlehem, be not afraid
For there you'll find, this happy morn
A princely babe, sweet Jesus, born.

With thankful heart and joyful mind
The shepherds went the babe to find
And as God's angel had foretold
They did our Saviour Christ behold
Within a manger he was laid
And by his side a virgin maid
Attending on the Lord of Life
Who came on earth to end all strife.

There were three wise men from afar
Directed by a glorious star
And on they wandered night and day
Until they came where Jesus lay
And when they came unto that place
Where our beloved Messiah lay
They humbly cast them at his feet
With gifts of gold and incense sweet.

We know very little about where the words to this song originated. The tune is simple, yet captivating. The words, too, simply recall the basic story of Jesus' birth. The rhythm of the tune seems conducive to walking, and the words seem to call us to walk alongside the pregnant virgin, the sleepy shepherds, and the "wise men from afar."

There are some books worth reading again and again. I started reading the *Hobbit* and the *Lord of the Rings* trilogy in graduate school, and I continue to read them each Christmas. It started out as a "reward" for reaching the end of the fall semester; it's more of a tradition now. Folks in my family used to ask me why I was reading them again, since I already knew how the story ended. It's probably a fair question…beyond the implication that I was somehow not normal….

The answer is two-fold. First, I very easily slip back into the fantastic and highly detailed narrative world Tolkien created. The narrative is still funny when it is supposed to be, and I still can't read about Frodo and Sam traveling in Mordor after dark. Secondly, and just as importantly, I still see something new or from a new perspective every time I read these tales.

There are many familiar and oft-told tales in our lives. This may be especially true of the stories of Jesus' birth and infancy. After all, we spend almost five weeks each year hearing them again. Sometimes the story runs the risk of being too familiar, and we run the risk of not listening very carefully. Our ears and our brains move on to the next word and the next scene, and we don't slow down enough to pay attention.

Most of us had a good idea where we were going when it came time to give birth to a baby. We knew just which hospital, and we had a plan worked out through multiple practice runs. We were not wandering through a strange region and town, made itinerant and homeless by governmental decree.

I suspect few of us have been startled in our place of work by a visit from an archangel, much less overwhelmed by the thunderous singing of an angelic choir. Ironically, it was fairly easy for these shepherds to find this particular baby; Jesus was probably the only child in the area using a feed trough for a cradle.

Even though the wise men had a star to guide their way, they still found themselves wandering in strange and foreign lands. In fact, we know that they missed their destination by about 10 miles the first time. They might still be wandering if the star hadn't reappeared when they were leaving Jerusalem to give them much better direction.

The Wexford Carol is a call to "consider well and bear in mind" this Advent season. It asks us to slow down to a stroll and stop running so frenetically. We are invited to come alongside these characters in the Christmas story and see their world from their perspective. And to remember what our "good God" has done for us in the birth of Jesus.

May God's Spirit clear our minds and help us listen. This day and every day. Amen.

Second Saturday in Advent

Of the Father's Love Begotten

Tune: DIVINUM MYSTERIUM (11th Century)
Words: Aurelius Clemens Prudentius (348-413)
Translator: John Mason Neale

Of the Father's love begotten
ere the worlds began to be,
He is Alpha and Omega;
He the source, the ending He,
of the things that are, that have been,
and that future years shall see
evermore and evermore!

O that birth forever blessed,
when a virgin, full of grace,
by the Holy Ghost conceiving,
bore the Savior of our race;
and the Babe, the world's Redeemer,
first revealed his sacred face,
evermore and evermore!

O ye heights of heaven adore Him,
angel hosts, His praises sing,
pow'rs, dominions, bow before Him,
and extol our God and King;
let no tongue on earth be silent,
ev'ry voice in concert ring
evermore and evermore!

Christ, to Thee with God the Father
and, O Holy Ghost, to Thee,
hymn and chant and high thanksgiving
and unwearied praises be:
honor, glory, and dominion,
and eternal victory
evermore and evermore!

The Fourth Century of the Christian era was a theologically contentious era. Well past the early energy of its founding years and secure in its cultural standing following Constantine's conversion, the Church of the Patriarchs gathered to debate theological boundaries. What constituted orthodox theological positions? What – and who – fell outside the lines of acceptability.

The nature of Jesus was central to those discussions. Was he fully divine? Fully human? Somehow fully both? What was his relationship to God the Creator and divine Parent? These are the years of creedal statements and excommunications. They saw arguments over differences represented by as little as one "iota" – that one letter making the difference between "same" and "similar" – when talking about the true essence of Jesus' nature. Approved creedal statements finally corralled orthodox positions, although they usually asserted – rather than explained – the Church's position.

The words written by a Spanish lawyer/poet of the turn of the 4th and 5th Centuries build on that orthodox position that Jesus is fully divine…of the same essence and nature with God. Jesus is co-equal and co-existent throughout eternal time. Like the creedal statements, the words of Prudentius offer no logical explanation for that mystery. But his words – set to an 11th Century chanting melody – explore that reality and some of its ramifications.

Like the prelude to John's Fourth Gospel, the opening verse asserts Jesus' existence prior to the beginning of creation. Jesus is not created; Jesus is "begotten." And Jesus' "begetting" is the result of God's overwhelming love. Jesus is beginning and end, the source of all past, present, and future creation. Neale's refrain ties all of the verses together: "evermore and evermore."

The early Church also spent considerable time and energy arguing over Mary's perpetual virginity. The second verse turns our attention to this "blessed virgin." It is something of a passing reference, though, giving most of its attention to her role as a pure vessel for the immaculate conception. Birth is not a beginning for the Savior. Birth is but the first time Jesus the Christ reveals his face.

Verse three shifts our attention to the Heavenly realms, where powerful voices of all types acknowledge Jesus as "God and King." They bow and sing his praises throughout eternity. And, in the fourth verse, we join our voices with theirs in a Trinitarian doxology.

One of the things we realize when we commit to listening to words like these is that the nature of Jesus is mysterious. To be both fully divine and fully human – at the same time – is an equation that won't compute. We can't explain it. We can only accept and affirm it as a choice through faith. For with God, and in God's love, nothing is or will be impossible.

May God's Spirit give us the grace and strength to see what is possible. This day and every day. Amen.

Advent Week Three

Joy

Third Sunday in Advent

Birthday of a King

Words and Music: William Harold Niedlinger (1918)

In the little village of Bethlehem,
There lay a Child one day,
And the sky was bright with a holy light
O'er the place where Jesus lay.

Refrain:
Alleluia! O how the angels sang.
Alleluia! How it rang!
And the sky was bright with a holy light,
'Twas the birthday of a King.

'Twas a humble birth-place, but O how much
God gave to us that day,
From the manger bed what a path has led,
What a perfect, holy way. [Refrain]

We are fascinated by origins. We want to know how and where things began. We put great stock in knowing when people were born and where they spent their early years. We are often genuinely interested in the other person's history, but there is also our sense that knowing such details somehow grants us special insight into another person's character and probable behavior. Those details help us fit other people into our understanding of the world around us.

Birthdays are one way we celebrate individual origins. They give us an excuse to feel "special" for at least one day in the year. Even though we share the day with others, our own day somehow belongs only to each one of us.

Niedlinger's song, written and published in a book of songs for children, reminds us that a "birthday" is something we share with

Jesus. We celebrate his birthday annually, giving each other gifts in imitation of God's gift of a Savior. Instead of "Happy Birthday," we imitate the angels and sing "glorias" and "alleluias" to mark the most holy of birth-days.

The song also evokes familiar images that reacquaint us with the stark contrast between the "holy light" and Jesus' humble birthplace. Niedlinger's refrain soars with the angelic "alleluias," offered to the holy family and the entire world in celebration of Jesus and his human beginnings. The song's concluding verse lifts our gaze to the "perfect holy way" that began at the manger.

We don't really know the date or year Jesus was born. What we do know is where he was born. Bethlehem was David's "hometown," and even though a descendant of that royal line had not occupied the throne in Jerusalem for many years, a descendant of David would always be heir to that throne. Bethlehem was the place of royal "origins," and God chose the little town to merge the royal with the divine at the point of Jesus' human "origins." It was the birthday of a king; it was the birthday of a messiah. It was the birthday of God incarnate.

No wonder the heavens "rang" with alleluias!

May God's Spirit be present with us this day and cause our hearts and voices to sing with joy as we remember Jesus' royal birth. And find us faithful. This day and every day. Amen.

Third Monday in Advent

Good Christian Men, Rejoice

Words: 4th Century Latin
Translator: John Neale
Tune: IN DULCI JUBILO

Good Christian friends, rejoice
with heart and soul and voice;
give ye heed to what we say:
Jesus Christ was born today.
Ox and ass before him bow,
and he is in the manger now.
Christ is born today!
Christ is born today!

Good Christian friends, rejoice
with heart and soul and voice;
now ye hear of endless bliss:
Jesus Christ was born for this!
He has opened heaven's door,
and we are blest forevermore.
Christ was born for this!
Christ was born for this!

Good Christian friends, rejoice
with heart and soul and voice;
now ye need not fear the grave:
Jesus Christ was born to save!
Calls you one and calls you all
to gain his everlasting hall.
Christ was born to save!
Christ was born to save!

The words to this song evoke visions of a group of carolers, dressed – perhaps – in Victorian clothes and strolling along a snow-covered residential street at dusk. At least that would be the Hallmark version. Whatever the picture, the words have both singers and audience in view.

The careful reader will also notice that I have followed many modern hymnals and chosen a version with updated words. I wanted to choose language that would be specifically inclusive, rather than presuming that the modern ear will hear "men" as generic language applying to everyone regardless of gender. And I rather like the idea of thinking of fellow Christians as "friends," no matter the level of personal acquaintance.

For the point of the words is a call to rejoice. To find intrinsic joy in the idea of Jesus' birth. And to do so with "heart," and "soul," and "voice." Like the words to other songs we hear and sing during the seasons of Advent and Christmas, this song begins with the good news of Jesus' birth and carries references to the bucolic manger scene. But verses two and three extend our reason for rejoicing to the good news of "endless bliss" and no longer needing to "fear the grave."

These words call us to sing with everything we are. But they also call us to remember why we are singing. We do not merely celebrate the birth of a baby born of the house and lineage of David. We celebrate the birth of one whose life and teachings offer eternal salvation. We joyfully proclaim the birth that irrevocably altered the cosmos and our very lives.

These words propel us out of the stable and into the streets. They ask us to sing and invite others to rejoice with us. For "Christ is born today/for this/to save."

May God's Spirit give us ears to hear and voices to sing from our hearts and souls. This day and every day. Amen.

Ding Dong Merrily on High

Words: George Ratcliffe Woodward (1924)
Tune: BRANLE DE L'OFFICIEL

Ding dong merrily on high,
In heav'n the bells are ringing:
Ding dong! verily the sky
Is riv'n with angel singing
Gloria Hosanna in excelsis!
Gloria Hosanna in excelsis!

E'en so here below, below,
Let steeple bells be swungen,
And "Io, io, io!"
By priest and people sungen
Gloria Hosanna in excelsis!
Gloria Hosanna in excelsis!

Pray you, dutifully prime
Your matin chime, ye ringers,
May you beautifully rhyme
Your eve'time song, ye singers
Gloria Hosanna in excelsis!
Gloria Hosanna in excelsis!

Hosanna in excelsis!!!

Some churches have clusters of bells which can be rung in sequence to play melodies. Some of these bell towers may be controlled by a computer; others are still rung by change ringers who control the swing of the bells through their arc with ropes and pulleys. Handbells were developed in the late 17th Century to offer the change ringers a chance to rehearse without disturbing the surrounding neighborhood. Many of us have played in a handbell choir, even in a church which has neither bells nor tower.

The words to this song imagine that the Heavenly bell towers rang with joyful abandon to herald the birth of Jesus, just as the sky was split wide open by the singing of the angelic hosts. And the bells ring out from church bell towers on Christmas Day to echo those heavenly bells. That joy is matched by clergy and lay alike, singing "Io" and "Gloria!" In the third verse, the song invites ("pray you") the ringers of the bells to play out throughout the day from morning until night. Ringing and singing "Gloria, Hosanna in the Highest!"

There is an unfettered joy present both in the words and notes of this song. The tune dances along, and the words seem to dance with their notes. The bells are swinging back and forth, pealing out their song. They call us to look upward to the heavens, split then with the song of the angels and now with our own song of "Gloria" and "Hosanna."

Today seems like a good day to dance and sing. For joy. Joy without boundaries. Joy without limits. Joy that somehow sounds like the ringing of Heaven's bells.

May God's Spirit fill our hearts and voices with joy as we celebrate the life of Jesus in our midst. This day and every day. Amen.

The First Noel, the Angel Did Say (vv. 1-2)

Anonymous Traditional English Carol

The first Noel the angel did say
was to certain poor shepherds in fields as they lay;
in fields where they lay keeping their sheep,
on a cold winter's night that was so deep.

[Refrain]
Noel, Noel, Noel, Noel,
born is the King of Israel.

They looked up and saw a star
shining in the east, beyond them far;
and to the earth it gave great light,
and so it continued both day and night.

[Refrain]

Noel is a modernized spelling of the older English "nowell," a transliteration of the French word "nouel." But that doesn't get us any closer to figuring out just what the word means. We might speculate a relationship with the Latin "*natalis*" (birth) or the French word "nouvelle" (new). Either one will get us close to the reason for using "noel" in relationship to the birth of Jesus, although they would signify slightly different angelic messages.

Perhaps we are better off allowing both meanings to reverberate in the words of the angels. Perhaps we are better off hearing the message that Jesus the Savior has been born coexisting with the announcement that God is doing something new in the world. They are, after all, both true. And they complement each other.

Like those of many other hymns and songs of Advent and Christmas, these words narrate the events surrounding Jesus' birth.

The first verse transports us to a cold and lonely hill on the outskirts of rural Bethlehem. We arrive just in time to hear and see the archangel and the heavenly chorus announce the "noel" to the shepherds "keeping" their sheep. The night is dark and "deep," and just now exploding with the glory of the angelic message.

Verse two transforms the light of angelic glory to another type of heavenly light: the star shining in the East. The shepherds wake – and look – up to see this brightly shining star. The star is itself a new thing, shining unusually brightly in the sky. And the star's brightness does not dim with the rising of the sun.

All kinds of new and unusual things are happening as the story unfolds. The song's refrain punctuates each new episode with its reminder that the "king of Israel" is born.

Finding the "new" in Advent and Christmas may be difficult. Finding the familiar and the comfortable is far easier; the familiar and comfortable provide much of the appeal of these seasons. But we cannot stand on Bethlehem's hill or look up into Bethlehem's night sky without acknowledging the "new" of these events. Or allowing them to be "born" anew each year.

May God's Spirit renew our lives in the joy and wonder of God's first "Noël." This day and every day. Amen.

Sing We Now of Christmas

Traditional French Carol
Tune: NOEL NOUVELET (15th Century)

Sing we now of Christmas,
Noel, sing we here!
Hear our grateful praises
to the babe so dear.

Refrain:
Sing we Noel, the King is born, Noel!
Sing we now of Christmas, sing we now Noel!

Angels called to shepherds,
"Leave your flocks at rest,
journey forth to Bethlehem,
find the lambkin blest." [Refrain]

In Bethlehem they found him;
Joseph and Mary mild,
seated by the manger,
watching the holy child. [Refrain]

From the eastern country
came the kings afar,
bearing gifts to Bethlehem
guided by a star. [Refrain]

Gold and myrrh they took there,
gifts of greatest price;
there was ne'er a place on earth
so like paradise. [Refrain]

Seasonal decorations are the rule in our household, and my wife usually handles the transition from one season to the other on her own. But decorating the house for Christmas has usually been an event reserved for the entire family, scheduled during the Thanksgiving weekend. Early in our marriage, my wife began collecting and displaying nativity scenes. Her collection is not as lavish or expensive as some, but there are nativities scattered throughout the rooms of the house. Many are unique, and all have a story.

The words of this traditional French carol engage the singers in their own nativity celebration. The crèche was a focal object of homes and town squares. The "inhabitants" of the crèche told their story annually. Their presence at Bethlehem's stable and manger provided an opportunity too good to be missed. Children and adults alike could participate in the telling of the Christmas story.

This carol might be sung around the crèche in the house. Or the townspeople might sing their song of Christmas as they processed to the town square or to the Cathedral. The words of this carol bring us familiar news of the birth of the Christ child. We sing – and hear – again of the angels and shepherds and wise men. At the same time, the lilting tune makes our feet dance as we sing. Words and notes alike invite us to join in a full-bodied celebration of Jesus' birth. We have difficulty being bystanders. We have to take our place in the crèche.

Perhaps the most important idea/word in this carol comes with its first line – "Sing *we* now of Christmas." Following Jesus has never been about standing in the wings or in the shadows. Following Jesus – from the very beginning – has been about taking our place at the manger and in the procession. We sing, we dance, and we rejoice….

May God's Spirit set our hearts to singing as we join the parade. This day and every day. Amen.

Third Friday in Advent

Angels We Have Heard on High

Traditional French Carol (18th Century)
Translator: James Chadwick (1813-1882)
Tune: GLORIA

Angels we have heard on high,
sweetly singing o'er the plains,
and the mountains in reply
echoing their joyous strains:

Refrain:
Gloria, in excelsis Deo!
Gloria, in excelsis Deo!

Shepherds, why this jubilee?
Why your joyous strains prolong?
What the gladsome tidings be
which inspire your heav'nly song?
[Refrain]

Come to Bethlehem and see
Him whose birth the angels sing;
come, adore on bended knee
Christ the Lord, the new-born King.
[Refrain]

See within a manger laid
Jesus, Lord of heaven and earth!
Mary, Joseph, lend your aid,
sing with us our Savior's birth.
[Refrain]

This is another carol which may have been popular in the French tradition of crèche celebrations. It references one of the most iconic scenes from Luke's infancy narratives, and words like "we" put us singers in the midst of that first holy night. We have heard angels singing "on high," with the earth ("the mountains") echoing their song "in reply." The refrain of "Gloria" is quoted directly from Luke's narrative.

The words of the next verse reveal that we didn't actually see the angels; we merely heard their song and its terrestrial echoes. On the other hand, we do see the shepherds. In fact, they appear to be parading past us and singing the "Gloria" taught them by the angelic choir. Their echo of the song invites us to follow them. To "come to Bethlehem" and witness the baby that inspired the angelic anthem. To worship "on bended knee" the new-born who is Christ and King.

Now we, like the angels and the shepherds, are singing "Gloria." We, like the shepherds, have arrived at the manger to witness and worship the Lord of Heaven and Earth. The Lord of angels and mountains. And Mary and Joseph are invited to "lend their aid," to sing "Gloria" with us.

Unlike the previous carol, these words do not set our feet to dancing and skipping. But these words and music invite us to join the parade. And the chorus. To let our voices soar with those of the angels and the shepherds and the holy family. And to bow our knees in worship with the strains of "Gloria" still ringing in our ears. Long after our voices have ceased to sing, the "Gloria" still bounces from house to house and mountain to mountain. Its echoes do not seem to die out. In fact, each echo seems stronger than the last.

We have heard heavenly angels. Their song is joyous and glorious. But more glorious still is the presence of the Lord of Heaven come to take up residence on Earth. To abide in our midst, full of glory and power and love.

May God's Spirit let "Gloria" ring out through our lives. This day and every day. Amen.

Third Saturday in Advent

Joy to the World! The Lord is Come

Words: Isaac Watts (1719)
Tune: ANTIOCH – G. F. Handel/arr. Lowell Mason

Joy to the world, the Lord is come!
Let earth receive her King!
Let ev'ry heart prepare Him room,
and heav'n and nature sing,
and heav'n and nature sing,
and heav'n, and heav'n and nature sing.

Joy to the earth, the Savior reigns!
Let men their songs employ,
while fields and floods, rocks, hills, and plains
repeat the sounding joy,
repeat the sounding joy,
repeat, repeat the sounding joy.

No more let sins and sorrows grow,
nor thorns infest the ground;
He comes to make His blessings flow
far as the curse is found,
far as the curse is found,
far as, far as the curse is found.

He rules the world with truth and grace,
and makes the nations prove
the glories of His righteousness
and wonders of His love,
and wonders of His love,
and wonders, wonders of His love.

It seems, perhaps, a little strange to be listening to the words of Watts' great hymn before Christmas Day. After all, we often sing this hymn as part of a Christmas Eve vespers service, rejoicing in the birth of Jesus the Christ child. But Watts' text is based on Psalm 98 and Genesis 3, not the events of the gospel infancy narratives. His words bring us back into the midst of the "in-between" of Advent.

These words call us to rejoice in the reality of Jesus' birth and reign. They call us to remember the effects of Jesus' incarnation. The Savior they have in view is no swaddled babe lying in Bethlehem's manger. He isn't even a toddler receiving the homage and royal gifts of Zoroastrian magi. This Jesus is Lord and King and Savior, ruling the "world with truth and grace."

These words do not transport us back in time to consider the events surrounding Jesus' birth. Instead, they allow us to testify to a present and future reality. To re-member the first Advent and celebrate its cosmic effects, all the while looking to the Advent of Jesus the Christ which is promised and not yet fulfilled. Each of the first three verses revolves around an imperative, the "let" which is more command than permission. "Let" both Earth and heart to make room for the Christ. "Let" human beings and nature alike sing out their joy. "Let" no more sin, sorrow, and thorns bedevil the creation, absolved from the "curse" by the blessing of God's only begotten Son.

The final verse affirms the reality of Jesus' eternal reign over the entire world and all of its "nations." A reign characterized by grace, truth, glory, righteousness, and wondrous love.

Both words and music send our voices and souls soaring. They sound our joy with robust gusto; we almost match the glory of the angelic chorus. But the joy of the world cannot be limited to that first Noël. The joy of Christ's birth, life, death, and resurrection echoes throughout eternity. How can we keep from singing?

May God's Spirit give us hearts and voices that repeat the sounding joy! This day and every day. Amen.

Advent Week Four

Peace

Fourth Sunday in Advent

O Little Town of Bethlehem

Text: Phillips Brooks (1868)
Tune: ST. LOUIS, Lewis H. Redner

O little town of Bethlehem,
how still we see thee lie!
Above thy deep and dreamless sleep
the silent stars go by.
Yet in thy dark streets shineth
the everlasting light;
the hopes and fears of all the years
are met in thee tonight.

For Christ is born of Mary
and, gathered all above,
while mortals sleep, the angels keep
their watch of wond'ring love.
O morning stars, together
proclaim the holy birth,
and praises sing to God the King,
and peace to men on earth.

How silently, how silently
the wondrous gift is giv'n!
So God imparts to human hearts
the blessings of His heav'n.
No ear may hear His coming,
but in this world of sin,
where meek souls will receive Him still
the dear Christ enters in.

The great American Civil War was over, and Phillips Brooks – Rector of Holy Trinity Episcopal Church in Philadelphia – had gone on pilgrimage to the Holy Land. The story behind these words is oft told; Brooks rode on horseback from Jerusalem to Bethlehem on Christmas Eve to worship at the basilica built over the traditional site of the Nativity. Along the way, he was struck by the quiet of rural and pastoral Bethlehem. He wrote the words a couple of years later for the children in his Sunday School. They were set to music by the parish organist.

The words portray a sleepy village seemingly unaware of the marvelous events that took place in its midst. They evoke a calm and quiet town, whose streets are now empty of any shepherds on a pilgrimage to see the newborn child. And whose skies hold only the distant echo of angelic voices. Only the morning stars continue to sing the heavenly "Gloria" and "Peace."

In the silence, Brooks experiences the presence of God, the "wondrous" gift of incarnation. His first verse has already mentioned the intersection of "hopes and fears" in these silent streets; the quiet and peace of Bethlehem is somehow God's benediction. And "meek souls" provide a fitting reception, a home for a Savior born in a humble stable.

The bloody conflict that had ravaged the United States was but one of the conflicts clawing at the fabric of late-18th Century life. Places of peace and quiet where one could experience God's benediction would be scarce over the next 100 years. In fact, one could argue that they remain scarce in our present day. We live in a world that seems bent on division. Frankly, were it not for music, we would experience little in the way of harmony.

Even the seasons of Advent and Christmas will overwhelm us with noise if we are not careful and vigilant. There is a healing balm in the peaceful quiet represented by Bethlehem and re-membered by these words. And the still, small voice of God speaking to our hearts.

May God's Spirit give us peace and the strength to be quiet. This day and every day. Amen.

Fourth Monday in Advent

God Rest Ye Merry, Gentlemen

Traditional English Carol (18th Century)

God rest ye merry, gentlemen
Let nothing you dismay
Remember, Christ, our Saviour
Was born on Christmas day
To save us all from Satan's power
When we were gone astray
O tidings of comfort and joy,
Comfort and joy
O tidings of comfort and joy

In Bethlehem, in Judah,
This blessed Babe was born
And laid within a manger
Upon this blessed morn
The which His Mother Mary
Did nothing take in scorn
O tidings of comfort and joy,
Comfort and joy
O tidings of comfort and joy

From God our Heavenly Father
A blessed Angel came;
And unto certain Shepherds
Brought tidings of the same:
How that in Bethlehem was born
The Son of God by Name.
O tidings of comfort and joy,
Comfort and joy
O tidings of comfort and joy

"Fear not then," said the Angel,
"Let nothing you affright,
This day is born a Saviour
Of a pure Virgin bright,
To free all those who trust in Him
From Satan's power and might."
O tidings of comfort and joy,
Comfort and joy
O tidings of comfort and joy

The shepherds at those tidings
Rejoiced much in mind,
And left their flocks a-feeding
In tempest, storm and wind:
And went to Bethlehem straightway
The Son of God to find.
O tidings of comfort and joy,
Comfort and joy
O tidings of comfort and joy

And when they came to Bethlehem
Where our dear Saviour lay,
They found Him in a manger,
Where oxen feed on hay;
His Mother Mary kneeling down,
Unto the Lord did pray.
O tidings of comfort and joy,
Comfort and joy
O tidings of comfort and joy

Now to the Lord sing praises,
All you within this place,
And with true love and brotherhood
Each other now embrace;
This holy tide of Christmas
All other doth deface.
O tidings of comfort and joy,
Comfort and joy
O tidings of comfort and joy

This venerable English carol seems much like the French crèche carols. We have no idea when it was written; it first shows up in printed form in the mid-18th Century, and it was common enough for Charles Dickens to refer to the carol in his *A Christmas Carol*. Like the crèche carols, its words tell the story of Jesus' birth, complete with angels, shepherds, and a manger.

Perhaps the minor key of the tune influences us, but these words envision a darker and more dangerous time. We cannot escape the opening contrast between the carol's wish for our merry-ness and its reference to salvation "from Satan's power." Perhaps we have once again found ourselves in the "in-between," since this birth means far less without the life, death, and resurrection that follows. Only in the realization that this baby is God incarnate, come to save the world from the power of evil, sin, and death, do we sing. Only in that reality do we have "tidings of comfort and joy."

Verses three and four envision the angels' announcement of the holy birth to "certain" shepherds, complete with the angelic admonition to "fear not." The angels come directly from God in Heaven to find these shepherds, and the news they bring is clear. The baby in the manger is God's Son, come to "free all those who trust in Him/from Satan's power and might." The next two verses picture a group of shepherds so excited by the news that they abandon their flocks to fend for themselves on a night characterized by "tempest, storm, and wind." When they arrive at the stable in Bethlehem, they find the baby. They also find Mary kneeling in prayer, the picture of piety.

The final verse admonishes all of the hearers ("in this place") to join with carolers in singing praises to God and the baby Jesus. In addition, it seems that "merry" gentlemen are to "embrace" each other in the spirit of "true love and brotherhood." But perhaps the most powerful line in the carol is its final assertion that the "holy tide of Christmas/All other doth deface." Powerful and inexorable, the message and spirit of Christmas overcomes everything that would frighten or threaten. Just as the work of Jesus the Christ overcomes all sin and death in eternal salvation.

The world has always been a scary place. There are times, it seems, when the threats seem larger and more imminent, but evil and its attendant darkness have always been a part of the cosmic order. But the refrain of this carol is still our response – "O tidings of comfort and joy…."

May God's Spirit fill your life with comfort and joy. This day and every day. Amen.

I Heard the Bells on Christmas Day

Words: Henry Wadsworth Longfellow (1864)
Tune, WALTHAM, by John Baptiste Calkin (1872)

I heard the bells on Christmas day
Their old familiar carols play,
And wild and sweet the words repeat
Of peace of earth, good will to men.

I thought how, as the day had come,
The belfries of all Christendom
Had rolled along th'unbroken song
Of peace on earth, good will to men.

And in despair I bowed my head:
"There is no peace on earth," I said,
"For hate is strong, and mocks the song
Of peace on earth, good will to men."

Then pealed the bells more loud and deep:
"God is not dead, nor doth He sleep;
The wrong shall fail, the right prevail,
With peace on earth, good will to men."

Till, ringing, singing on its way,
The world revolved from night to day
A voice, a chime, a chant sublime,
Of peace on earth, good will to men.

Some of the most stirring poetry arises from lives stricken with deep and abiding tragedy. Henry Wadsworth Longfellow is a famous American poet of the 19th Century, and his poems often relate epic stories connected to the American experience. But this poem, later fashioned into a hymn by J. B. Calkin, emanated from a dark time in Longfellow's life. His wife had been killed in a freak household accident, burned to death when her dress caught on fire. Longfellow suffered burns to his hands and face attempting to put out the fire. That same year – 1861 – the country plunged into its Civil War, and Longfellow's son defied his father to join the Union army. His son was severely wounded in 1862.

By 1864, the country was reeling from devastating battles, and Longfellow's words reflect an America struggling to find hope. The church bells still rang out across the nation's towns on Christmas day, marking the day of Jesus' birth with what was meant to be a joyful sound. One wonders if the use of those bells to toll the deaths of young men over the past few years had imbued their sound with slightly more gravity than joy for those still living at home. Longfellow understood the "story" in their ringing on this day, though. The bells tolled their "familiar carols" and told a story of peace on earth that was both "wild and sweet." Longfellow also remembered a day when the bells of churches tolled their story around the world without ceasing.

The next verse of the hymn seems abrupt in its picture of the author bowing in "despair." The original poem has two other verses which were omitted from the hymn text. In those verses, Longfellow "heard" the rolling sound of cannon away to the south, their thundering mouths drowning out the ringing of the bells and their carol of peace and good-will. And their "earthquake" shaking the very "hearth-stones of a continent"…making "forlorn" all too many households.

No wonder the poet bowed his head in despair. Sometimes grief and loss are too difficult to bear. The good folk of the nation were continuing to "hate" and kill each other in the name of God. Where was God in this fight, when those on every side claimed God's blessing for their cause?

Somehow, the poet raised his head to listen more intently…and heard the bells sound "more loud and deep." God was not dead; God was not even asleep. God was present in spite of human attempts to obliterate "peace" and "good-will" from the face of the Earth. Wrong would not prevail against right. The last verse of the hymn reinforces the realization of God's ongoing presence, with the bells – and their message of hope and peace – unsilenced. It is a "chant sublime" proclaiming God's grace and providence.

Many of us live our lives without being touched by such deep and abiding tragedy. We rejoice in births and grieve the loss of deaths, but those are normal events in human living. Normal or not, though, we all face events which suggest that God has abandoned us and our world. The power and presence of evil continues...seemingly unabated. Evil is local; it is global; it is cosmic. And we are forced to acknowledge its reality.

But we are not forced to give in to its claim to power. If there were no other meaning in Advent and Christmas, there would still be the message of God's overwhelming love and grace. It is a message that comes not with the loud pealing of church bells, but in the quiet cry of a newborn baby. It is in the anguished words of a parched Jesus, admitting his feeling that God had forsaken him just before forgiving those who crucified them. It continues in the quiet words of the angels in Easter's garden and in the blessing of the risen Savior. God is with us. We are not alone.

May God's Spirit give us grace and peace...and strength for the living of these days. This day and every day. Amen.

What Child is This?

Author: W. Chatterton Dix (1837-1898)
Tune: GREENSLEEVES

What Child is this, who, laid to rest,
On Mary's lap is sleeping?
Whom angels greet with anthems sweet,
While shepherds watch are keeping?

Chorus:
This, this is Christ, the King,
Whom shepherds guard and angels sing:
Haste, haste to bring Him laud,
The Babe, the Son of Mary!

Why lies He in such mean estate,
Where ox and ass are feeding?
Good Christian, fear: for sinners here
The silent Word is pleading.[Chorus]

So bring Him incense, gold, and myrrh,
Come, peasant, king to own Him.
The King of kings salvation brings;
Let loving hearts enthrone Him.[Chorus]

The tune is hauntingly familiar; it is only an Advent/Christmas tune for having been used for the words of Dix's hymn. The words of the first verse and the chorus combine the scenes from Luke's birth narratives in Chapter 2, as our nativity tableaux usually do. Here is the homely scene from the stable: the baby being held by Mary, the shepherds and animals stationed down stage, and the angels floating above and slightly to one side. They are just waiting for the magi and their camels to appear and take their appointed places. Which they will do by verse three.

The question – what child is this? – could be asked by any one of the members of the tableau. And even more so by those of us looking on/in. The scene is beyond fantastic; the events narrated by Luke and Matthew are credible only if we accept the witness of those shepherds and angels and magi. Jesus's beginnings are almost too humble. The rise from stable to palace, from feedbox to throne, is almost too much of a stretch. Particularly when that throne is located in Heaven. Like Mary, we have some pondering to do. Like all of the characters in Luke's story, we put our faith and our credibility in the assertion of the angel Gabriel that nothing will be impossible with God's involvement.

The chorus answers the questions of the first two verses. This child is the Messiah – the "Christ" – King, Lord, and Savior. Still "babe," still "son of Mary," but also Son of God. And we, like the angels, shepherds, and Magi, "haste" to laud him. The admonition to good Christians to "fear" probably calls us to an attitude of reverence and worship than to one of terror.

Like the Magi, we bring gifts, whether we are peasant or king. We acknowledge the Christ as King, Lord, and author of salvation. We offer our very beings as throne for Jesus's reign. Our vantage point allows us to see the newborn baby, the crucified man, and the glorified Lord at the same time. We can understand the ways in which the God-incarnate bridges the gap between manger and throne, between stable and Heavenly palace. We see for ourselves the truth of the angel's assertion. God is with us…and nothing is impossible anymore.

May God's Spirit give us eyes and ears of faith. And find us aithful. This day and every day. Amen.

Fourth Thursday in Advent

Away in a Manger

Anonymous (19th Century)

Away in a manger, no crib for a bed,
the little Lord Jesus laid down His sweet head;
the stars in the heavens looked down where He lay,
the little Lord Jesus asleep on the hay.

The cattle are lowing, the Baby awakes,
but little Lord Jesus, no crying He makes.
I love Thee, Lord Jesus, look down from the sky
and stay by my side until morning is nigh.

Be near me, Lord Jesus; I ask Thee to stay
close by me forever and love me, I pray.
Bless all the dear children in Thy tender care,
and fit us for heaven, to live with Thee there.

This carol is a familiar one for children. The first two verses were likely written for children to sing in Sunday School, somewhere around 1885. And the third verse was probably added a few years later when the song was published in a second collection. Its prayer is slightly out of sync with the first two stanzas, but the addition of such a prayer is very much in line with trends in the latter part of the 19th Century.

The words seem so simple. Somewhere far away – both in time and space – the little baby Jesus lay down to sleep in a manger. Since, of course, he had no crib "for a bed." All is peaceful under the stars until the "lowing" cattle wake the baby up. The next few words continue the peaceful scene, but they picture the "ideal" baby of someone's imagination. After all, most healthy babies do not wake from sleep without crying. This picture is reminiscent of the idealized and stylized images of the Madonna and Child, with the baby Jesus seated on the lap of Mary – both of them crowned with halos of light – holding the fingers of his hand in the triune benediction. The quiet and hyper-aware baby of this carol is more the risen Lord than a realistic picture of a newborn baby.

But we are, after all, still in the in-between of Advent. And we really cannot look at the baby Jesus without seeing Jesus the adult…and Jesus the eternal. There is something very comforting about remembering that Jesus experienced the human life cycle. That experience guarantees empathy, not just sympathy. God "with us" in the flesh, not just in the spirit.

That is the prayer bound up in this children's song that still speaks to us as adults. We pray that Jesus the Christ – child, adult, and risen Lord – would stay "by our side." We pray that he would watch over all of God's children with "tender care." We ask that he "fit us for heaven."

We are all too aware that it doesn't have to be dark to be "night" in our world. Our need for peace, and for a lullaby, is no longer confined to bedtime. We long for calm and security. And we find our rest in the presence of God and under the tender watch-care of God's only begotten Son.

May God's Spirit renew our ability to experience God's peace and rest. This day and every day. Amen.

Fourth Friday in Advent

It Came upon the Midnight Clear

Words: Edmund H. Sears (1849)
Tune: CAROL (Willis, c. 1850)

It came upon the midnight clear,
that glorious song of old,
from angels bending near the earth
to touch their harps of gold:
"Peace on the earth, good will to men,
from heaven's all-gracious King."
The world in solemn stillness lay,
to hear the angels sing.

Still through the cloven skies they come
with peaceful wings unfurled,
and still their heavenly music floats
o'er all the weary world;
above its sad and lowly plains,
they bend on hovering wing,
and ever o'er its Babel sounds
the blessed angels sing.

And ye, beneath life's crushing load,
whose forms are bending low,
who toil along the climbing way
with painful steps and slow,
look now! for glad and golden hours
come swiftly on the wing.
O rest beside the weary road,
and hear the angels sing!

For lo! the days are hastening on,
by prophet seen of old,
when with the ever-circling years
shall come the time foretold

when peace shall over all the earth
its ancient splendors fling,
and the whole world send back the song
which now the angels sing.

This very familiar Christmas carol makes no mention of the Christ child or most of the events surrounding Jesus' birth. Rather, the hymn's words focus on the angelic chorus and their "glorious song of old." The poetry evokes a crystal-clear winter's night…and an almost brittle stillness. It is as though the world was holding its breath waiting for angels to announce the "all-gracious" God's message of "peace."

Subsequent verses of the hymn, however, shift their focus from that first "midnight clear" to the present. God is still sending a message of peace and goodwill, and the angels still "come with peaceful wings unfurled" through the "cloven sky." But the world no longer waits in silent anticipation. Instead, its "sad and lowly plains" are filled with "Babel" sounds. Human beings still toil and labor, bent over "beneath life's crushing load." The picture is not pretty. Peace, goodwill, and harmony were not the order of the day in the mid-19th Century when Edmund Sears penned these words. The social fabric of his time was torn by poverty and violent political division.

Would that our world felt much better 150 years later. We human beings insist on repeating our mistakes, and human history is all too easily characterized by the phrase "wars and rumors of wars." Poverty, sickness, and violence continue to plague our world. The wealthy too often continue their oppressive ways, and we would rather raise violent voices than loving arms. We react – and interact – with fear, with ill- instead of goodwill. And peace eludes us….

It would be easy to throw up our hands and abandon any responsibility for our lives and those around us. It might even make sense to escape inwardly, becoming hermits in our own minds and ignore the seemingly hopeless situation we seem not just to have inherited but even encouraged.

The Season of Advent strongly reminds us, though, that we live between the "already" and the "not yet." Our best hope lies in the conviction that God's message of peace and goodwill continues in the voices of the angelic chorus. We share that hope with Edmund Sears, for the tenor of his poem abruptly changes in the middle of the third verse. The song calls us weary travelers to look up and see that "glad and golden hours come swiftly on the wing." The last verse of the carol continues that incredibly hopeful outlook, remembering that prophets foretold not only the initial advent of Jesus the Christ and our Savior, but a glorious time "when peace shall over all the earth its ancient splendors fling, and the whole world send back the song which now the angels sing."

Our annual Advent journey always wraps us in this fabric. Hope, love, joy, and peace were long ago woven together by an "all-gracious" God. It is our security blanket, and we should not fool ourselves into thinking that somehow we don't need it or have outgrown it. The world of the in-between is too threatening to face without remembering the power of God's love demonstrated in the first advent of Jesus. That love compels us to love each other fiercely. It calls us to share the blended light of Advent's four candles, shining with hope and love and joy, weaving all together into the peace that lies within us, among us, and in front of us, even when the how or why passes our understanding.

May the song of God's peace enfold us. And may God's Spirit cause our voices to join together and echo back the angels' song of God's peace and goodwill! This day and forever more. Amen.

Fourth Saturday in Advent

Dona Nobis Pacem (Canon)

Words: Traditional, Latin
Tune: DONA NOBIS PACEM (Round)
Latin (English translation: "Give us peace.")

Dona nobis pacem, pacem.
Dona nobis pacem.
Dona nobis pacem.
Dona nobis pacem.
Dona nobis pacem.
Dona nobis pacem.

G ive us peace.

Perhaps these words have always been a profound prayer. Tragically, human history seems too easily characterized by war and discord, not peace. Just as tragically, too often the only hope for peace would be an answer to prayer.

That prayer is spoken or sung by Christians around the world as we gather for the Eucharist. The words conclude the final line of the *Agnus Dei* (Lamb of God): *Agnus Dei, qui tollis peccata mundi, dona nobis pacem* (Lamb of God, who takes away the sins of the world, grant us peace.). The *Agnus Dei* has probably been part of the Latin mass since the 7th Century CE, and it is also part of the Service of the Eucharist in most Protestant liturgical traditions.

This particular setting, using only the prayer for peace, has its roots somewhere in the oral tradition of the church. The musical setting is a canon, or round, in three parts. As each part enters, the harmonies build. By themselves, both the text and the musical canon are deceptively simple. Combined, they have incredible power.

"Give us peace."

The Season of Advent has drawn to a close; the Season of Christmas is upon us. Before the clock chimes and the calendar page flips, though, these simple words and their powerful prayer remind us again that Advent is the Season of the in-between. We have been preparing to welcome the Christ-child into a world that was troubled by war and violent oppression. We have always known that the manger's baby would be crucified and raised from the dead. Good Friday's cross and Easter's resurrection are the inevitable end of the story begun in Advent. Our salvation is accomplished, yet our world is still troubled by war and violent oppression. So we still pray, for God's peace, for we know that God's peace is our hope for this day and for eternity.

May God's Spirit be ever present in our midst…and grant us peace. Now and forever. Amen.

Section Two

Listening through Christmas

Christmas Eve (December 24)

Silent Night! Holy Night!

Words: Joseph Mohr (1816), translated by John F. Young
Tune: Franz X. Gruber (1818)

Silent night, holy night
All is calm, all is bright
Round yon Virgin Mother and Child
Holy Infant so tender and mild
Sleep in heavenly peace
Sleep in heavenly peace

Silent night, holy night!
Shepherds quake at the sight
Glories stream from heaven afar
Heavenly hosts sing Alleluia!
Christ, the Savior is born
Christ, the Savior is born

Silent night, holy night
Son of God, love's pure light
Radiant beams from Thy holy face
With the dawn of redeeming grace
Jesus, Lord, at Thy birth
Jesus, Lord, at Thy birth"

Few Christmas songs are as familiar as these words and their simple tune. Written by a poor assistant priest in Austria, then set to a melody composed by the church's cantor, these words have a resonance that stretches over two centuries. They transport us to the quiet stable, peaceful in the aftermath of all of the hubbub. Mary and Joseph and baby Jesus have settled in following the visit of the shepherds and their tale of angelic singing. The baby is finally asleep, and the exhausted parents can rest.

Luke's Gospel narrative tells us that Mary "pondered" the events of the evening "in her heart" (Luke 2:19). They are certainly events worth remembering and pondering. Stables and mangers might have been within the range of normal for someone in Mary's and Joseph's socio-economic class. Her "Magnificat," did, after all, center around her lowly status and relative poverty. But angelic choirs announcing the baby's birth to third-shift shepherds would appear to be outside of anyone's definition of ordinary. I doubt that Mary and Joseph were expecting shepherds to find them in the stable and come for a visit so soon after Jesus' birth.

The words of the song help us to ponder the events, too. "Shepherds quake" and "glories stream" while "heavenly hosts sing alleluia." They are a good summary of the evening's events on the hills outside of Bethlehem, and the impact of the angelic presence throughout Luke's narrative has not lessened over the millennia.

We need not ponder long to reach the same conclusion as the song. This is no ordinary baby, no matter how humble the circumstances of his birth. This is the culmination of Gabriel's announcement to Mary some months before. God's only Son has been born, and the world has been turned upside down. True Love and Light has entered creation in a way we could scarcely contemplate; "redeeming grace" is not only a possibility but a reality.

Had we been there with Mary and Joseph and the shepherds, we would probably not have seen radiant beams emanating from the baby as he lay asleep in the manger. But there is poetic license for the eyes of faith. For this person is God's advent in human flesh. Light and Life are his purview. Dawn has come to overcome the night. Jesus…Lord at birth, Lord at death, Lord at resurrection, Lord forever.

May God's Spirit bathe our lives in the light of God's redeeming grace. This day and every day. Amen.

Christmas (December 25)

O Come, All Ye Faithful

Words and Music: John F. Wade (c. 1743)
Translator: Frederick Oakeley
Tune: ADESTE FIDELUS

O come, all ye faithful, joyful and triumphant,
O come ye, O come ye to Bethlehem!
Come, and behold Him, born the King of angels!

Refrain:
O come, let us adore Him;
O come, let us adore Him;
O come, let us adore Him, Christ, the Lord!

God of God, light of light,
Lo, he abhors not the Virgin's womb;
True God, begotten, not created [Refrain]

Sing, choirs of angels; sing in exultation;
sing, all ye citizens of heav'n above!
Glory to God, all glory in the highest! [Refrain]

Yea, Lord, we greet Thee, born this happy morning;
Jesus, to Thee be all glory giv'n!
Word of the Father, now in flesh appearing! [Refrain]

Christmas morning is here. Our waiting for the advent of the Christ-child is over. The baby is in the manger and wide awake, ready for the faithful to come and visit. And worship. So, the words of this hymn call us to the parade of the faithful. With others around the world and through the ages, we make our way – "joyful and triumphant" – to "Bethlehem."

Why have we come? To see the newborn baby, born "King of angels!" And to "adore" him, "Christ the Lord." The song's refrain brings us back to that singular focus of adoration, of worship. Here, then, is the benefit of being "in-between." We know how this part of the story will finish as we watch its beginning unfold. Here is no ordinary baby, and we have not come merely to wish him and his parents a long and fruitful life. We have not come for a short visit to share just a moment of parental pride and acknowledge how cute the newborn is.

We are here to worship. To pay our homage to the one who is "God of God, light of light." To join our voices with all those throughout the ages who have echoed these affirmations of the Nicene Creed. Who find in this child a true equality with God the heavenly Parent. God eternal; Light eternal; "begotten, not created."

And, it seems, we are here to sing. To sing exultant words, soaring words in concert with "choirs of angels." To sing our "Gloria" again and glorify God with our song and our lives. And to "greet" Jesus, our Lord and Savior, "born this happy morning." The only-begotten "Word of the Father" appearing enfleshed, abiding with human beings for just a while. Our songs of wonder have been transformed into songs of praise, and we join our voices with all of the saints and the company of Heaven.

We sing a song of praise, adoration, and worship this day. But we also sing a song that calls us to action. We sing the song of the "faithful," called together to be God's people in the world. Called together to praise, adore, and worship Jesus the Christ not just with our words but with our very lives.

May God's Spirit pour all of the blessings of hope, love, joy, and peace upon us this Christmas Day. And find us faithful. This day and every day. Amen.

December 26

Go, Tell it on the Mountain

Traditional Spiritual
Collated and Arranged by John W. Work, Jr.

Refrain:
Go, tell it on the mountain,
Over the hills and everywhere;
Go, tell it on the mountain,
That Jesus Christ is born.

While shepherds kept their watching
O'er silent flocks by night,
Behold, throughout the heavens
There shone a holy light. [Refrain]

The shepherds feared and trembled,
When lo! above the earth
Rang out the angel chorus
That hailed the Savior's birth. [Refrain]

Down in a lowly manger
The humble Christ was born,
And God sent us salvation
That blessed Christmas morn. [Refrain]

Let's be honest. Sometimes the season of Advent and the run up to Christmas Eve and Christmas Day leaves us exhausted. We have focused all our energy toward making it to Christmas, and we just want to spend the next few days trying to recover. The season of Advent gives us any number of opportunities to adopt a less frenetic pace, but we still have difficulty slowing down and listening.

Part of our problem is a tendency to consider Christmas to be the goal – the finish of our celebration – rather than the beginning. Our culture pushes us in this direction, encouraging us to start our preparation for Christmas earlier each year. But we also fall into a familiar pattern, with Christmas coming "after." After all of the year's other holidays. After all the parties and school programs. After Advent. The culmination of the time of celebrating. A sign that the calendar year and the fall semester of the school year is over. But the liturgical year is still very young. After all, we just began a new liturgical year – a new "church" year – with the first Sunday of Advent. We are celebrating birth; the rest of our liturgical attention will be given to life and ministry…and passion, death, and resurrection. The season of Lent will be upon us before we know it, as our year of study and worship re-members and re-lives the cycle of Jesus' earthly life.

So, what are we to do? If we consider Christmas to be a beginning, we follow the example of those in the Gospel narratives. We go and tell. The words of today's song give us a start. They remind us of Luke's story. Simple shepherds surprised by angelic visitation – a "holy light." Frightened and shaking, they – like their fellow peasant Mary just a few months before – encountered God's messengers with an amazing message.

Most of us can identify with the characters in Luke's narrative. Few of us would consider ourselves extraordinary. Our self-image has more in common with the humble peasants in the story – Mary, Joseph, the shepherds. Even Zechariah the priest and his wife Elizabeth are not portrayed as persons at the center of Jerusalem's power structure. They are the "poor" who will be "filled," while the "rich" are "sent empty away." The cosmos has been turned upside down by the birth of God's only begotten Son. Hope and love and joy and peace have been born anew, wrapped in bands of cloth, and laid in a Bethlehem manger.

We – like the shepherds and Jesus' earthly parents – have been given both task and opportunity. We have been called to "go" and "tell it on the mountain." There is "good news," and we are its messengers. We cannot…and should not…keep quiet. There is telling and singing and living to be done. It can be a scary thought; this calling to tell out the good news is not always a comfortable calling. We tend to forget that we are not called to accomplish salvation or persuade others to follow Jesus. We have been called to tell the good news. To proclaim the incarnation of God's salvation. To introduce others – by word and deed – to Jesus the Christ whom we know and follow.

If the shepherds could do it, perhaps we can, too.

May God's Spirit give us strength and courage for the living of these days. And find us faithful. This day and every day. Amen.

December 27

Gentle Mary Laid Her Child

Words: Joseph S. Cook (1919)
Tune: TEMPUS ADEST FLORIDUM

Gentle Mary laid her Child
Lowly in a manger;
There He lay, the undefiled,
To the world a stranger:
Such a Babe in such a place,
Can He be the Savior?
Ask the saved of all the race
Who have found His favor.

Angels sang about His birth;
Wise men sought and found Him;
Heaven's star shone brightly forth,
Glory all around Him:
Shepherds saw the wondrous sight,
Heard the angels singing;
All the plains were lit that night,
All the hills were ringing.

Gentle Mary laid her Child
Lowly in a manger;
He is still the undefiled,
But no more a stranger:
Son of God, of humble birth,
Beautiful the story;
Praise His name in all the earth,
Hail the King of glory!

Things are beginning to settle down. We are a couple of days into the season of Christmas, and we see some minor signs of normalcy. Today's words return us to the manger and stable, but the stable is quiet. Mary and Joseph and the baby have become a part of the normal stable scene, save for the fact that the manger is still functioning as Jesus' crib. Perhaps there are other feed troughs in the stable, or the normal occupants have adapted to the new normal by eating off the ground.

The rest of Bethlehem and Judea and the Roman Empire has also returned to normal. In fact, the birth of this baby in rural Judea has hardly caused a hiccup in the wider world. The newborn Jesus is a "stranger" to the great majority of his contemporaries. The events surrounding his birth are quickly fading into distant memory, and they were fantastic enough that they seem almost like holy hallucinations. The idea that the newborn baby lying in a manger is God's Son seems so incongruous and unlikely that it raises the question admitted by the words of the song: "could this be the Savior?"

The answer comes from those who follow the risen Lord, from those who have found God's favor in the blessing of God's salvation. The answer comes with the memory and the recitation of those marvelous events. In the retelling of the Gospel's story. In the re-membering of the angels' song and the shepherds' witness and the wise men's visit.

The last verse is an affirmation of faith. Gentle Mary's child is still "undefiled," but no longer a stranger. His "humble birth" has born the promised fruit of God's salvation. And we add our voices to those of the angels and the shepherds and the Magi. We, too, tell his "beautiful" story and hail him as the "King of glory."

May God's Spirit guide us in a world flipped upside down. And give us the strength and courage for the living of these days. This day and every day. Amen.

O Holy Night

Words: Placide Cappeau (1847)
Translated by John Sullivan Dwight (1855)
Tune: CANTIQUE DE NOËL, Adolphe Adam (1847)

O holy night, the stars are brightly shining,
It is the night of the dear Savior's birth;
Long lay the world in sin and error pining,
'Till he appeared and the soul felt its worth.
A thrill of hope the weary world rejoices,
For yonder breaks a new and glorious morn;

Chorus
Fall on your knees, Oh hear the angel voices!
O night divine! O night when Christ was born.
O night, O holy night, O night divine.

Led by the light of Faith serenely beaming;
With glowing hearts by his cradle we stand:
So, led by light of a star sweetly gleaming,
Here come the wise men from Orient land,
The King of Kings lay thus in lowly manger,
In all our trials born to be our friend;

Chorus
He knows our need, To our weakness no stranger!
Behold your King! Before Him lowly bend!
Behold your King! your King! before him bend!

Truly He taught us to love one another;
His law is Love and His gospel is Peace;
Chains shall he break, for the slave is our brother,
And in his name all oppression shall cease,
Sweet hymns of joy in grateful Chorus raise we;
Let all within us praise his Holy name!

Chorus
Christ is the Lord, then ever! ever praise we!
His pow'r and glory, evermore proclaim!
His pow'r and glory, evermore proclaim!

Written by the town wine merchant and poet, this song celebrated a refurbished church organ. Its words focus less on the particulars of the Christmas scene than the emotions surrounding our understanding of the event. They evoke a sense of awe not always conveyed by the songs and hymns of Christmas. The tune – especially the soaring chorus – is a memorable setting for these words.

Sometimes a winter night is clear and cold, and on those nights the stars seem to shine even brighter. Their light seems as crisp as the evening. There is a feeling of clarity and expectation on such nights, and the words of the song's first verse capture that. We contemplate the birth of Jesus, and we are lifted out of our world which has been "pining" in "sin and error" awaiting just such a moment. The "thrill of hope" is in the air. Like the shepherds we fall to our knees on such a holy night.

The second stanza invites our approach to the stable and manger. With the shepherds…and then the Magi…we are guided by "the light of Faith" to find the holy child. We recognize Jesus as both Lord and friend. The "normal" circumstances of his birth and early days mark him as someone who can relate to us, not just to the professional clergy or the highly placed in society. Jesus understands our trials and our needs. Again, the chorus exhorts us to worship the one who is no stranger "to our weakness."

The words of the third verse are different from most of the songs we have listened to this Advent and Christmas. They probably reflect a growing discomfort in the mid-19th Century with political and economic oppression. Societal rumblings raised questions about slavery and suffrage, about inalienable rights and social responsibility. The words of the song call us to follow Christ's example of love for each other. They warn us that Jesus the Christ will break the chains of bondage and slavery, for "the slave is our brother." In response, we sing "sweet hymns" in "grateful Chorus," praising the "Holy name" of Jesus and proclaiming his "pow'r and glory evermore."

There is a clarity and hope that accompanies such a radical call to love and justice. It is perhaps too easy, especially at this time of the year, to reduce our perception of Jesus the Christ to a meek and mild baby boy, living in humble circumstances. We have become so familiar with the story that we lose some of the shock and awe of the angelic visitation to the shepherds and the thunder of the angelic chorus. We are so comfortable with words like salvation and redemption that we may forget for just a minute that these blessings come from God only through the suffering and death of the very child we are fussing and cooing over as he lies in Bethlehem's manger.

Even though Christmas has come, we still live in the in-between. In fact, since Christmas has come, we follow the light of our own faith and do our part to fight and defeat all manner of oppression. With renewed hope and peace and joy and love. With the presence and grace of our Lord and Savior...who is also friend and brother. God is with us. We are not alone. Thanks be to God.

May God's Spirit give us the necessary strength and courage for the living of our days. And find us faithful. This day and every day. Amen.

December 29

Let All Mortal Flesh Keep Silence (vv. 3-4)

Words: Liturgy of Saint James
Tune: PICARDY

Rank on rank the host of heaven
spreads its vanguard on the way,
as the Light of light descendeth
from the realms of endless day,
that the pow'rs of hell may vanish
as the darkness clears away.

At His feet the six-winged seraph,
cherubim, with sleepless eye,
veil their faces to the Presence,
as with ceaseless voice they cry,
"Alleluia, alleluia!
Alleluia, Lord most high!"

We are in waiting mode again. The star has appeared, but the Magi will have a long journey to make to pay their homage to this new "king" of the Jewish people. Our liturgical calendar will compress their trip into about twelve days, and we celebrate the season of Christmas on our way to Epiphany. These days are another "in-between," a reminder that we still live and move and have our being between the two advents of Jesus the Christ.

The last two verses of "Let All Mortal Flesh Keep Silence" are not very silent. Stanza three pictures "rank on rank" of the heavenly "host," lined up in battle formation. They are the "vanguard" preceding Jesus as he comes/returns in victory to finish off cosmic evil. As the "Light of light" descends from Heaven to vanquish the powers of Hell and drive out darkness with eternal light.

103

Stanza four takes us to the Heavenly throne room. Angelic beings –
cherubim and seraphim – spend their eternal days in ceaseless vigil
at the foot of Jesus' throne. With eyes "veiled" in the presence of
such holiness, their song, too, is never-ceasing: "Alleluia!"

Frankly, the words and music of these final verses of the song build
to a powerful climax. We lift our voices with those of the angels to
sing "Alleluia" to the "Lord most high." Our alleluias fill the globe
as they echo those of the heavenly throne room. And it's thrilling!

Christmastide renews and re-energizes us for the work ahead. Since
we are still in the in-between. Since there is still work and worship
to be accomplished while we await the second advent of Jesus the
Christ. Since there are still songs to be sung and words to be heard
and hugs to be hugged and tears to be shed and smiles to be smiled.
Since there is still life to be lived in the presence of the one who is
both Bethlehem's baby and Heaven's Lord.

May God's Spirit give us strength and courage for the living of these
days. And find us faithful. This day and every day. Amen.

December 30

O Come, O Come, Emmanuel (vv. 3-5)

Tune: Veni, Emmanuel (Chant)
Translated (Latin): John Mason Neale (1851)

O come, Desire of nations, bind
All peoples in one heart and mind;
Bid envy, strife and quarrels cease;
Fill the whole world with heaven's peace.

Refrain:
Rejoice! Rejoice! Immanuel
shall come to you, O Israel.

O come, O Key of David, come
and open wide our heavenly home.
Make safe for us the heavenward road
and bar the way to death's abode.
[Refrain]

O come, Thou Day-spring, come and cheer
Our spirits by Thine advent here;
Disperse the gloomy clouds of night,
And death's dark shadow put to flight.
[Refrain]

These are dangerous words. They invite the presence of Jesus the Christ into our midst with all of the wonderful – and potentially challenging – consequences of that presence. We need to hear and pay careful attention to what we are requesting, so that we can be ready and willing to engage with Jesus as he turns creation upside down.

Perhaps every human generation has felt as if "envy, strife, and quarrels" was an apt description of the world's circumstances. We seem incapable of living with one another in peace and harmony.

The history of humanity is littered with "strife" at every level of human interaction. We learned long ago that only divine intervention will provide anything close to a solution. The third stanza of this ancient song pleads for the advent of Jesus, our "God with us"/Emmanuel. We seek the presence of God in our midst to "bind all peoples in one heart and mind" and to "fill the whole world with heaven's peace."

The horrible irony is that those of us who claim to follow the way of Jesus, who claim the name "Christian," have too often been the instigators of "envy, strife, and quarrels." We have rejected peace as a strategy. We need only look to ourselves and our own actions to understand just how broken our world remains. There may be no real solution during the "in-between" – on this side of the second advent – but God's presence in our midst will continue to challenge us to be true followers of the one who came to be our Peace.

The fourth verse invites the presence of God's Christ to open and safeguard our passage from this world to the next. Our choral prayer is that the "Key of David" would give us access to the promise of salvation for the "house" of David. We pray for eternal salvation, as well as safety and security along the way.

The final verse of the ancient song is a plea for God's light – God's "Day-spring" – to be present with us. Not just eternally, but in our present. To bring light that will drive away both our cosmic darkness and our worldly darkness. To "cheer our spirits" and "disperse the gloomy clouds." These words recognize the ever-present "shadow" of death in our existence. They yearn for the presence of Jesus in our midst to "put to flight" that "dark shadow." Now and for all eternity.

Each of these verses has been punctuated by the song's refrain. By the song's call for us to "rejoice" in the promise of God's presence. That promise which Jesus' birth fulfilled, and Jesus' death and resurrection confirmed. We do rejoice in the presence of God with us, even as we recognize God's call to be faithful servants. Faithful to God's vision, rather than to our own.

May God's Spirit bring us grace and peace. And find us faithful. This day and every day. Amen.

December 31

Once in Royal David's City

Words: Cecil Frances Alexander (1848)
Tune: IRBY, Henry John Gauntlett (1868)

Once in royal David's city
stood a lowly cattle shed,
where a mother laid her baby
in a manger for His bed:
Mary was that mother mild,
Jesus Christ, her little child.

He came down to earth from heaven
who is God and Lord of all,
and His shelter was a stable,
and His cradle was a stall:
with the poor, and meek, and lowly
lived on earth our Savior holy.

And our eyes at last shall see Him,
through His own redeeming love;
for that child so dear and gentle,
is our Lord in heav'n above,
and He leads His children on
to the place where He is gone.

Not in that poor lowly stable,
with the oxen standing by,
we shall see Him, but in heaven,
set at God's right hand on high;
when like stars His children crowned
all in white shall wait around.

This song is very familiar as the processional hymn for the annual service of lessons and carols at Kings College, Cambridge. Originally written to teach the catechism to children, the words to the song pick up the themes of Luke's infancy narrative and the ancient hymn of Philippians 2. Yes, these events took place in "royal David's city." But they were by no means "royal" beginnings.

The first verse echoes creedal language, affirming that Jesus was 'born of the virgin Mary.' The words of the second stanza picture the descent of God's only begotten Son – "God and Lord of all" – from the heavenly realms to his earthly sojourn. Jesus the Christ 'humbled himself…taking on the form of a servant,' dwelling for a little while in human form "with the poor, and meek, and lowly."

The last two verses shift our perspective. Here is Bethlehem's baby now risen Lord of Heaven. Now "our eyes at last shall see him." The vision of faith will finally recognize Jesus and understand the trajectory of his life. The humble stable is merely the beginning of Jesus' journey to save humanity. Having provided cosmic redemption, Jesus now leads God's children into the heavenly realms. Bethlehem's stable fades into the background, and our vision clearly shows us Jesus seated at the right hand of God the Parent. Attended by God's children "like stars…crowned all in white."

It would be nice to be able to romanticize these words and leave them in their mid-19th Century context, alongside Victorian-age street urchins and workhouses for the poor. That context might make us feel better about words that appear designed to give hope to the working poor and a sense that there was a better life awaiting them in Heaven. For all of our social and technological advances, however, despair and poverty are still too prevalent in our world. Too many people experience food and housing insecurity. Too many still consider their relative wealth to be the result of God's blessing for their righteous and pious behavior instead of the result of income inequalities built into the socio-economic system.

The words of this song provide hope for all of us. After all, we are all in need of the redemption provided through Jesus' incarnation. But they also challenge us to proclaim a good news that connects spiritual realities with physical realities. Jesus came to offer salvation

– true peace and a sense of security. Jesus came to challenge us to love one another as he loved us.

May God's Spirit give us strength and courage for the living of these days. And find us faithful. This day and every day. Amen.

January 1

The First Noel, the Angels Did Say (vv. 3-5)

Anonymous Traditional English Carol

And by the light of that same star
three Wise Men came from country far;
to seek for a king was their intent,
and to follow the star wherever it went.

Refrain:
Noel, Noel, Noel, Noel,
born is the King of Israel.

This star drew nigh to the northwest,
o'er Bethlehem it took its rest;
and there it did both stop and stay,
right over the place where Jesus lay. [Refrain]

Then entered in those Wise Men three,
full reverently upon the knee,
and offered there, in his presence,
their gold and myrrh and frankincense. [Refrain]

For many years our church staged a Live Nativity just before Christmas. Since its beginnings were connected with the youth department, many of the recurring roles – Mary, Joseph, shepherds, angels, and wise men – were usually played by members of the youth group and some of their friends. We set up a sound system and lights and other props, such as Elizabeth's "house" and Bethlehem's stable, on the hill and parking lots adjacent to the church building. The archangel Gabriel had his perch, and a star was mounted over the stable's roof.

By the time our family became involved, the Associate Pastor (responsible for youth, music, and a host of other activities) had been setting up, staging, and directing the event for many years. He and I had many discussions about the setup, since he would periodically look for ways to vary the script and presentation. One of those discussions concerned the arrival of the Magi. Neither of us was quite happy with the traditional crèche scene, even though it almost ensured that a picture would find its way into the local newspaper. Ponder as we might, though, neither of us could figure out a way to make the transition from the stable – with its animals and shepherds – to some sort of house where Mary, Joseph, and the holy toddler could receive the visit of the Magi two or three years later. There just wasn't enough room on the hill or time in the presentation.

The last three verses of this song use the star to make that transition. In the first two verses, the shepherds experience an angelic announcement about the baby's birth and see a star "that gave great light." Now, "the light of that same star" provides a guide for astrologers (Magi or "Wise Men") from a far country who "seek a king" by following the star "wherever it went." The Magi didn't actually follow the star from their home to Jerusalem. Being learned astrologers, they correctly interpreted the rising of the star to herald the birth of an heir to the Judean throne. They made their way to Herod's court to offer their congratulations and their gifts. Imagine their surprise to find no young royal heir living in the palace. Once they were pointed to Bethlehem, though, they were able to follow the star and find Jesus and his family.

I wonder if the appearance of the Magi surprised Mary and Joseph as much as the shepherds' visit did that first night. I doubt that they appeared as outlandish as our Hollywood-informed imagination pictures them in most nativity scenes and presentations. They were likely weary and worn from their long journey, and they probably hadn't been received with lavish hospitality at the palace in Jerusalem. They had traveled to Bethlehem to recognize the new king and bring gifts worthy of royalty. The song's final stanza names the gifts of gold, myrrh, and frankincense.

Midway through the season of Christmas we begin a new calendar year. As artificial as the turning of a calendar page may be, there is always a sense of hope that the new year offers exciting opportunities. These astrologers from the east had correctly interpreted the appearance of a special star. A star that promised a new era, a new generation. They acted on that promise, bringing gifts fit for a royal heir. More than that, though, they brought the gift of their own action. The gift of their journey.

May God's Spirit guide us along our journey and God's presence be the only star we need to find our way. This day and every day. Amen.

January 2

Angels from the Realms of Glory

Words: James Montgomery (1816)
Tune: REGENT SQUARE, Henry Smart (1866)

Angels from the realms of glory,
wing your flight o'er all the earth;
ye who sang creation's story
now proclaim Messiah's birth:

Refrain:
Come and worship, come and worship,
worship Christ, the newborn king.

Shepherds, in the field abiding,
watching o'er your flocks by night,
God with us is now residing;
yonder shines the infant light: [Refrain]

Sages, leave your contemplations,
brighter visions beam afar;
seek the great Desire of nations;
ye have seen his natal star: [Refrain]

It happens for me every year. We come to the point in the liturgical calendar and in the lectionary texts when it is time for someone to read the words of Luke 2. Since most of my life has a soundtrack, there is usually some sort of music running in my head if I stop to listen. The soundtrack to Luke 2 is usually from Handel's *Messiah*, especially when the angel appears to the shepherds along with the angel chorus. The archangel's words finish the soprano's recitative…just in time for the conductor's downbeat. And the angel chorus sings its fortissimo "Glory to God in the highest!"

The words to Montgomery's hymn convey a similar thrill and excitement. The first stanza reminds us that these same angelic

113

beings have been singing in God's presence from the beginning, and their songs of praise to God rang out at the moment of creation. With their appearance on the hills outside of Bethlehem, the heavenly throne room has relocated to earth, even for a short while. And they sing "Messiah's birth."

The refrain calls us to join with the angels. To "come and worship."

The second and third stanzas issue a similar call to the shepherds of the fields and the distant sages. Verse two speaks to the shepherds "in the field abiding." Things have changed; "God with us is now residing." They, too, must leave their flocks and "come and worship." Verse three calls the sages to leave their "contemplations" and "seek the great Desire of nations," since "brighter visions beam afar." The "natal star" calls them to "come and worship," as well.

I imagine that Handel's powerful chorus is but a poor imitation of the angelic choral offering. In fact, I suspect that our attempts to "come and worship" are also something of a poor imitation of the worship and praise offered by the cherubim and seraphim surrounding God's throne. But that will not stop us from singing. Rather, their example will encourage us to song and praise and worship.

May God's Spirit put a song in our hearts and on our lips. And find us faithful. This day and every day. Amen.

January 3

Come, Thou Long Expected Jesus (v. 2)

Words: Charles Wesley
Tune: HYFRYDOL

Born thy people to deliver,
born a child and yet a King,
born to reign in us forever,
now thy gracious kingdom bring.
By thine own eternal spirit
rule in all our hearts alone;
by thine all sufficient merit,
raise us to thy glorious throne.

God with us. A consistent message of the Hebrew Scriptures is the growing separation of God from God's people. From the time the first humans disobeyed God and refused to take any responsibility for doing so, human relationships – with God, with creation, with each other – have been strained. We cultivate distance while craving intimacy. We foster unethical and immoral behavior, often without being fully aware we are doing so. We struggle to become faithful in our relationship with God.

God with us. As the words to the final stanza of Wesley's hymn assert, God is with us in the form of a baby born "a child and yet a King." Born to deliver God's people and bridge the chasm between God and God's creation. It was, as Mary reminded the archangel, an impossible task. But only impossible, as the archangel replied, without taking the power and presence of God into account.

God with us. Child and King born to "reign in us forever." Born to "rule in all our hearts alone," and "raise us to thy glorious throne." Jesus, the long-expected Messiah, whose birth and death and eternal life hold the power to accomplish these humanly-impossible cosmic tasks. Jesus, the long-awaited Messiah, whose "all-sufficient merit" holds the only power necessary to restore the relationship between

God and humanity.

God with us. "Incarnation" sounds so much more theological…and just a little out of our cognitive reach. After all, a perfect union of divine and human seems only possible through the agency of God. Even then, it seems like an incredible stretch. Even for a loving God.

God with us. On purpose. Thanks be to God!

May God's Spirit give us the strength and courage to love God and each other. This day and every day. Amen.

January 4

We Three Kings of Orient Are

Words and Music: John H. Hopkins, Jr. (1863)

We three kings of Orient are;
bearing gifts we traverse afar,
field and fountain, moor and mountain,
following yonder star.

Refrain:
O star of wonder, star of light,
star with royal beauty bright,
westward leading, still proceeding,
guide us to thy perfect light.

Born a King on Bethlehem's plain,
gold I bring to crown him again,
King forever, ceasing never,
over us all to reign. [Refrain]

Frankincense to offer have I;
incense owns a Deity nigh;
prayer and praising, voices raising,
worshiping God on high. [Refrain]

Myrrh is mine; its bitter perfume
breathes a life of gathering gloom;
sorrowing, sighing, bleeding, dying,
sealed in the stone-cold tomb. [Refrain]

Glorious now behold him arise;
King and God and sacrifice:
Alleluia, Alleluia,
sounds through the earth and skies. [Refrain]

Most of the songs of Advent and Christmas draw their content from Luke's infancy narratives. They tell the story of Mary's encounter with the archangel. They sing of shepherds and angels and Bethlehem's quiet streets. They picture the baby Jesus, swaddled and lying in a manger. These are the most enduring images of the Christmas season. Images of the crèche, complete with star and Magi.

But the story of the star and the Magi who "follow" it comes from a different Gospel. Matthew's infancy narratives have no stories of shepherds and angelic choruses. There are no stables and mangers, no picturesque tableaux of the holy family surrounded by oxen, donkeys, sheep, and shepherds. Matthew's is a story of dreams and prophecy. Of a New Testament Joseph and seemingly shattered marital hopes…until the angel of the Lord comes to this Joseph in a dream and lays out God's new plan.

Matthew's is a story of Babylonian astrologers observing a special star and choosing to travel almost a thousand miles to bring gifts to the Judean court, recognizing and celebrating the birth of a son and heir to the Jewish throne. And an uncomfortable scene in Jerusalem, as everyone is surprised by the news of a royal toddler. Ancient prophecy points the Magi toward Bethlehem, and the star appears again to guide them to the holy family. God's warning comes in dreams; the Magi escape back to Babylon and the east, while the holy family flees to Egypt. And Herod's soldiers slaughter innocent children.

Were there just three Magi? Matthew's Gospel only mentions three "gifts": gold, frankincense, and myrrh. From that, I suspect, we usually infer three Magi. Hopkins' song is organized around these three gifts, one from each wise man. Verse one introduces the three wise men, weary from a long journey from the "orient," and terms them "Kings." It's a nice image, but their place in ancient courtly society was probably more in line with priests or soothsayers. Zoroastrianism – one of the religions of ancient Babylon – observed and interpreted the movements of the stars and planets to gauge cosmic intent and its effect on humanity. Our picture of sumptuously dressed royalty coming to pay homage to the infant Jesus seems a little over the top.

The next three verses pick up on the meaning of the three gifts. Gold for a royal crown, a universal symbol of wealth and prosperity worthy of a king. Frankincense, a symbol of prayer and praise to the divine. And myrrh, a strong perfume used in the process of preparing a body for burial. These are "death" gifts, the kinds of gifts presented to royal babies with the understanding that a royal child ought already to have everything necessary for his earthly life. Death was another matter, though, and even kings needed gold to pay their way in the afterlife, incense to offer prayers for eternity, and perfume to mask the smell of decomposition.

The gifts would have been fitting for Herod's son. They were, perhaps, even more fitting for Jesus, as they acknowledged a life's task that would only be completed in death…and resurrection. The final verse shifts our focus to the resurrection. To the glory of the risen Christ: "King and God and sacrifice." To the "eternal light" whose presence causes Alleluias to ring "through the earth and skies."

May God's Spirit bless us along our journey, as we lay our gifts at the feet of the one who is both Bethlehem's toddler and Heaven's Lord. And find us faithful. This day and every day. Amen.

January 5

As with Gladness Men of Old

Words: W. Chatterton Dix (1858)
Tune: DIX (Kocher)

As with gladness men of old
did the guiding star behold;
as with joy they hailed its light,
leading onward, beaming bright;
so, most gracious God, may we
evermore be led to Thee.

As with joyful steps they sped
to that lowly cradle-bed,
there to bend the knee before
Him whom heav'n and earth adore;
so may we with willing feet
ever seek Thy mercy-seat.

As they offered gifts most rare
at that cradle rude and bare;
so may we with holy joy,
pure, and free from sin's alloy,
all our costliest treasures bring,
Christ, to Thee, our heav'nly King.

Holy Jesus, ev'ry day
keep us in the narrow way;
and, when earthly things are past,
bring our ransomed lives at last
where they need no star to guide,
where no clouds Thy glory hide.

In that heav'nly country bright
need they no created light;
Thou its Light, its Joy, its Crown,
Thou its Sun which goes not down;
there for ever may we sing
alleluias to our King.

Matthew's infancy narrative observed that the Magi were "overwhelmed with joy" when they saw that the star they had been following from Jerusalem stopped over the house in Bethlehem where the holy family was residing. That joy, that "gladness" is a fitting way to complete our listening journey through the season of Christmas.

The Magi had good reason to be worried at what they thought was the end of their journey from their home in the east. They had made their way to Jerusalem, since the star they observed announced the birth of the "king of the Jews." By any logic, such a child should have been living in Herod's palace among his royal household. It's easy to imagine everyone's shock and discomfort. Herod was notoriously paranoid and uncertain of his right to rule. The news from these Babylonian astrologers must have triggered considerable anxiety on his part. The court's religious authorities were certainly aware of the ancient messianic prophecies and their connection to the traditional home of the Davidic line.

But the wise men set out for Bethlehem without knowing much more than the ancient prophecies. Thankfully, they would get better guidance for this last segment of their journey; the star, itself, would lead them from palace to home. Dix's hymn opens with that joyful journey as the Magi followed the star's guidance – "leading onward, beaming bright." And the first stanza ends with a prayer that we might always be led toward our "most gracious God." The second verse pictures the travelers with "joyful steps" quickening their pace to reach the side of the "lowly cradle-bed." There they made their obeisance, bending the knee to "Him whom heav'n and earth adore." The prayer which ends the second stanza is a call for our own "willing feet" to seek God's "mercy-seat."

The final three verses of the song shift the focus to our own behavior. Verse three mentions the gifts brought by the Magi to the Christ-child, terming them "gifts most rare." But then "joy" of this stanza is our "holy joy" in presenting our own "costliest treasures" to Jesus the Christ. The fourth stanza is a prayer that Jesus would "keep us in the narrow way" in this world and bring us safely to the place where "our ransomed lives" have no need of a "star to guide." And the final verse describes that "heav'nly country bright" where the Light that is Jesus shines forever, and choruses of angels and human beings sing eternal "alleluias."

There are times when it would be nice to have a shining star of our very own, guiding us precisely to our goal. But our experience suggests that we will rarely, if ever, get such specific instructions. Like the Magi, we will need to undertake most of our journey as a matter of faith. We will see a distant "star," interpret its meaning correctly, and begin our steps accordingly. And it will only be at the end of our journey when the destination will become clearer and more precise.

Unlike the Magi, however, we have the advantage of Scripture and a "great cloud" of trailblazing "witnesses" to testify about their own journey. We have God's Spirit within and among us. God is with us on our pilgrimage, and we journey with glad joy!

May God's Spirit give us grace and strength for the journey. And find us faithful. This day and every day. Amen.

www.ingramcontent.com/pod-product-compliance
Lightning Source LLC
Chambersburg PA
CBHW071014120626
46546CB00003B/1077